T0094973

Tigers of the Sea

ROVERS OF THE DEEP

White Shark, Hammerhead Shark, Southern Ground Shark, Tiger Shark,
Spot-fin Ground Shark, Sand Shark, Loggerhead Turtle

Tigers of the Sea

Shark Fishing Around the World

Hugh D. Wise

THE DERRYDALE PRESS
Lanham and New York

THE DERRYDALE PRESS

Published in the United States of America
by The Derrydale Press
A Member of the Rowman & Littlefield Publishing Group
4720 Boston Way, Lanham, Maryland 20706

Distributed by NATIONAL BOOK NETWORK, INC.

© 1937 by The Derrydale Press
First Derrydale paperback edition 2003

Library of Congress Control Number: 2002112036
ISBN 1-58667-088-3 (pbk. : alk paper)

∞™ The paper used in this publication meets the minimum requirements of
American National Standard for Information Sciences—Permanence of
Paper for Printed Library Materials, ANSI/NISO Z39.48–1992.
Manufactured in the United States of America.

DEDICATION

TO MY WIFE WHO, FOR THIRTY YEARS, HAS
PATIENTLY BORNE WITH THE VAGARIES OF A
SPORTSMAN AND TO MY MOTHER, WHO BORE
WITH THEM FOR THIRTY YEARS BEFORE THAT,
I AFFECTIONATELY DEDICATE THIS BOOK.

ACKNOWLEDGMENTS

WITH GRATEFUL APPRECIATION TO MANY FRIENDS WHO HAVE HELPED ME ACCUMULATE DATA AND ESPECIALLY TO DOCTOR E. W. GUDGER, ASSOCIATE CURATOR, AMERICAN MUSEUM OF NATURAL HISTORY, TO PROFESSOR ULRIC DAHLGREN, PRINCETON UNIVERSITY, AND TO MR. E. N. SCHUETZ, NASSAU N. P., BAHAMAS.

MY THANKS ARE ALSO DUE TO PROFESSOR J. DUNCAN SPAETH, OF PRINCETON, FOR HIS VALUABLE CRITICISM OF THE MANUSCRIPT.

PREFACE

A COMPENSATION for hardships and uncertainties of active Army Life is the opportunity it affords for sport with rod and gun in many parts of the world. I have taken full advantage of this but I omit here discussion of all but shark-fishing.

Quite by accident, as a little boy on the Virginia Coast, I dropped into this unusual and exciting sport, and I have since pursued it at home, in Cuba, in the Philippines, in Hawaii and in the Bahamas.

Quite by accident, also, I found that shark-fishing could be fine heavy-tackle angling, and it is of that which I have tried to tell here. My accounts of experiences are limited to a few of those which I believe illustrate phases of the sport and show peculiarities of species most likely to be encountered in our waters.

This being a rather unusual game, it has seemed well to go into some detail as to methods and tackle used, and also to tell of salient peculiarities of this monster about which so little is generally known. Therein has been my greatest difficulty—to give the sportsman what he may wish to know without going unnecessarily deep into the classification and taxonomy of sharks.

If I have made mistakes, as I undoubtedly have, I stand ready for correction. If my methods and tackle can be improved upon, and I know both are far from perfect, I will welcome suggestions. Nevertheless, I hope that other sportsmen may find something useful in this book. At least, in writing it, I have accomplished something for myself because describing the fish has made me know them better, explaining methods and tackle has put my ideas in

order, and in recounting incidents I have lived them over again, and
I have had a bully time doing it—

Tight Lines!

HUGH D. WISE

Princeton, New Jersey,
July 25, 1936.

CONTENTS

CONTENTS

LIST OF ILLUSTRATIONS

LIST OF ILLUSTRATIONS

TIGERS OF THE SEA

Courtesy of Captain Lancaster

TIGRESS—NO RACE SUICIDE HERE
A viviparous female and her pups born after her capture

Courtesy of Dr. E. W. Gudger

WHALE SHARK
Taken at Acapulco, Mexico, 1935

CHAPTER I

ON ROD AND REEL

AMONG my first recollections of the sea is a tall sharp dorsal fin cutting along in the wake of the schooner pilot boat, "Phantom," outside the Virginia Capes while I stood by Captain Joe Darling, at the wheel, and listened to his yarns about sharks. When we lay-to, taking aboard a pilot from an outgoing ship, the sailors who wanted the hide of that shark for sandpapering decks, caught him on a rope handline. He came aboard with jaws snapping and eyes glaring, and I realize now that it was at that moment that I accepted the challenge of the monster to a combat which has lasted through years.

When the trout enthusiast grows eloquent, some deep-sea angler is likely to ridicule his "minnows" and then the fly expert derisively retorts that the heavy-tackle man should go to the pasture and hook onto a steer. Neither extremist finds any merit in the game of the other, the one choosing to see no sport in contest with weak little adversaries, the other considering only brute strength necessary to conquer a sea monster.

As a matter of fact, however, both play about the same game, for the tackles they use balance their fights with the fishes, so the struggle with a trout on a three-ounce rod is not necessarily incommensurate with that against a swordfish on heavy tackle and, if skill and experience are required in outwitting a trout, so are both needed to properly present the bait to a swordfish.

Even the despised handline has its fine points. Recently, I was

[1]

on the Chesapeake Bay in a boat with a rod expert and an eminent professor, incidentally a national authority on fish and fishing. We were after sharks but at suppertime we went to angling for food fish. The rod man stuck to his fine tackle and was steadily feeding peeler-crab to the elusive little "spots," repeatedly winding in to find that they had stolen his bait, but the deft forefinger of the professor, with humbler tackle, invariably hooked his fish, and it was he who provided our evening meal. When the professor had caught all the fish we needed, the rod man, who had caught none, remarked: "There *is* something to this handline game!"

This contention among fishermen, and in fact among all sportsmen, as to the relative merit of their games, antedates civilized records and doubtless the Neanderthaler quarrelled with his kind about the ethical method of snatching fish by the tail from prehistoric swamps. Coming on to our early fishing classics, we read in Isaac Walton's *Compleat Angler* (1653) a discussion between a Rider to Hounds, a Falconer and an Angler. None of these sportsmen seems to have been able to see merit in games other than his own and the Angler finally, after having heard what the others had to say, retorts, "I shall be glad to exercise your attention with what I say concerning my own recreation."

So, here, three hundred years later, though not advocating shark-fishing as the finest angling, I am asking for its recognition as a worthy sport and, really, in this I am fairer than was Isaac Walton for I make no invidious comparisons of different kinds of angling, while he said:

> I care not, I, to fish the seas,
> Fresh rivers best my mind do please.

[2]

To a man who loves all fishing, it seems entirely unnecessary to discredit one kind in order to extol another—I have had lots of fun catching chub when the trout would not rise, and I can enjoy even crabbing when the bluefish do not bite.

It is as useless to argue about what kind of fishing is the best sport as it is to contend as to the relative merits of athletic games. Trout fishing, bass fishing, and swordfish angling are as different as golf, tennis, and football, and, like those games, each is played according to its own rules, under its own code of ethics, and with its own special equipment. One does not play tennis with a baseball bat nor catch swordfish on a fly rod. It is equally absurd to dispute as to the best kind of fish to catch, for we might as well argue whether chicken or beef is better to eat—both are good.

I am writing all this to forestall the question, "Why does one wish to catch sharks?" for no sportsman who has had the thrill of struggles in the South Seas with Broadbills, Marlins and Yellow Fins (notice, I used capitals with their names) will compare the shark with them as a game-fish. The point is that the shark is often more convenient to our door and we may as well have fun with him, too. Although the shark of our North Atlantic Coast usually runs smaller than those I have caught in Cuba and the Philippines, he is big enough to furnish grand sport and, though not so lively as the sailfish nor so athletic as the Tarpon, he is about as strong as a mule and as hard to kill as a cat.

Big Game Fish

In considering shark-fishing as a sport, it is interesting to compare it with angling for some of the more popular deep-sea fishes.

[3]

The Tarpon, appropriately called "The Silver King," is much smaller than most pelagic sharks, the rod and reel record being less than two hundred and fifty pounds, but no fish enjoys the reputation of more glamourous fighting on the line. He rarely uses his entire strength in the water for he is essentially a "sky-rocket" taking to the air the moment the hook is driven with repeated amazing leaps in his efforts to throw it. Really, this is his undoing for the skillful angler has only to keep himself composed, to maintain his line taut, to humor comparatively short rushes and to wait for the fish to exhaust himself.

The Swordfish, included in which group are Broadbills and Marlins, is another leaper, a veritable "jumping-jack," but, he is also a "torpedo" on the surface and under it—capable of long terrific rushes, any sudden checking of which would mean disaster to the best of tackle, for these great fishes sometimes weigh five hundred or even a thousand pounds.

The capture of the "Royal Purple of the Sea" is probably the greatest test of angler's skill, involving as it does, the matching of strength of tackle against power and speed of fish, and the meeting of wild leaps into the air and of skittering on the surface.

Quite different from the struggle with the Swordfish but, nevertheless, a real test for the angler is the fight put up by a big Tuna, for he is fast, powerful, stubborn and amazingly enduring.

The Hawaiian Tuna, the Yellow Fin, is livelier though smaller than the great Blue Tuna of our North Atlantic Coast, which attains a weight of more than a thousand pounds, but he frequently leaps, while the Blue Tuna rarely does.

The Blue Tuna is more of a mule than a race horse but, nevertheless, he has bursts of tremendous speed. When he is not making one of these rushes, he is lying back against the line and subjecting it to all the strain it can bear or forcing the rod man to slip line to save it. Or he may sound deep and resist all efforts to lift him. Then, like a flash, off he goes in a reel-heating rush. Even though he may not have made a single leap before he is brought to gaff, he will have convinced the angler that he is a game-fish.

Somewhat like the Tuna's tactics are those of the pelagic Shark. Quite as speedy as the Tuna and even more powerful and more stubborn, he is also a past master at sounding. It is hard to realize that any fish could put up a more dogged resistance than does the shark, nor that any creature could display greater tenacity. He rarely leaps, and his runs, though more powerful than those of the Tuna, are likely to be shorter. There is little of the spectacular in the struggle with him and it is possible that it is the satisfaction of battering down such determined opposition which gives the thrill. A friend who once watched me for three hours in the swivel chair, pumping, slipping line, holding, gaining, losing, asked—"Do you call that fun?" "Yes," I replied. "It *is* fun." But I cannot say exactly why.

These four great sea fishes fight in quite different ways, but the outstanding characteristics which make angling for them attractive are: the spectacular gymnastics of the Tarpon, the amazing speed of the Swordfish, the tremendous power of the Tuna, and the savage tenacity of the Shark.

"With none of them," says the trout fisherman, "does one get the quiet beauty of sun-lit glade and purple shadow. There is no woodsy smell. There is no music of tinkling cataract on limpid stream along which, daydreaming, one forgets the world in his love of nature."

"No," replies the sea-fisher, "but I have the surge of the ocean.

I feel the bound of the boat. I inhale the breath of the sea and I taste the salt spray. It is action—life!"

Sharks are not generally classified as game-fishes but this arbitrary rule of fishing clubs, few of whose members have ever played the game with sharks, does not modify the excitement of the sport nor does it lessen the skill and understanding necessary to come through a shark fight with unwrecked tackle.

WHY FISH FOR SHARKS?

It is a poor way to start this story with the acknowledgment that the quarry sought is not equal, as a game-fish, to some others. I hope this admission may not be interpreted as discrediting the sport of angling with rod and reel for sharks, fishes whose vitality, stubbornness and power compensate for other qualities which they may lack. They really are worthy antagonists in struggles the interest of which is enhanced by the joy of combat with savage monsters. To bring them to gaff requires skill and judgment, and there are moments of breathless suspense though, except in struggles with the South Sea "Mako," with which my experience is very limited, there is not the sustained excitement which there is in a battle with a swordfish. Mackerel sharks often leap but usually a shark fights under water where he saves his strength for a powerful struggle instead of wasting it in useless though spectacular aerial gymnastics.

After all, however, one must acknowledge that the abundance of the game and the comparative inexpensiveness of its pursuit add materially to the attractions of shark-fishing.

The sportsman officer, often stationed near our greatest game fields and our finest fishing waters, is apt to be spoiled by the ease

and economy of his indulgence in sport. Of hunting this was, perhaps, more true a generation ago but, of deep-sea fishing, much developed in recent years, it is now especially true.

Some of us still like to make human derricks of ourselves, but
we are no longer stationed in the South Seas and we can no longer
have soldiers to go fishing with us for the fun of it. We must now
travel to fishing grounds, charter a boat and hire a crew, as do our
civilian friends, so the more accessible and less expensive shark-
fishing is acceptable to us as it should be to them.

In the *Literary Digest*, October 20, 1934, Mr. Dudley Giddell
says that each swordfish taken with rod and reel off Montauk that
summer represented an average cost of $3,571. This was the esti-
mate of Mr. Arthur Howe, Secretary of the Montauk Yacht Club,
which enjoys almost a monopoly of the Broadbill game there and,
yet, in 1932, only twelve Broadbills were taken there, eight in 1933,
and, up till October, 1934, seven.

On our Atlantic seacoast, therefore, the pursuit of the swordfish
is extremely uncertain and while that of the tuna is less expensive
and more reliable, it too is largely dependent upon opportunity. The
shark, however, so numerous as to be a nuisance on most fishing
grounds, greedily awaits your bait and his killing will be applauded
by the fishermen.

WHAT RODS MEAN TO THE SPORTSMAN

A great obstacle which anglers put in the way of their enjoy-
ment is their own stubborn insistence on making comparisons of
sport with different fish—the idea that some particular game-fish
is superior to all others and that he alone is worth angling for. Each

fish calls for different technique and different tackle. Each rod in the rack on my study wall brings to me memories of joyous days when it was the weapon used and anticipations of days when it will be used again.

The little three-ounce Leonard shoots out, over dark spots on the boiling sun-lit stream, a bright lure to be seized by the leaping speckled beauty. As I fondle it I can see the swirling rapids, hear the gurgling water, feel the gentle breeze through overhanging boughs, smell the scent of pines and even taste that trout, crisped over hickory embers.

The five-ounce Montague goes with me in the boat after bass, tugging jumping bull terriers of Lake Ontario where clear water, gravelly bottom and rocky shore make a luxurious setting—the fisherman in an armchair and a guide to bait his hook and to net the fish. Or, will it be for "Lakers" and walleyed pike on crystal lakes as beautiful as any in Switzerland?

With this trolling-rod come memories of days on the noble St. Lawrence, a French-Canadian guide babbling folklore in broken English while we hunted for muskallunge.

Off the Jersey coast, I've taken lots of bluefish on this split-bamboo and, with light rod and six-strand line, there are few gamer fish. This shorter rod was for channel-bass at Cape Charles and tarpon at Corpus Christi. The surf-rod was for "Stripers."

Here is my light tuna-rod. What visions it calls up of sparkling bounding blue seas, of surge of big fish and of fights to land them?

And, daddy of them all, heavy artillery in this review, my swordfish-rod! With it I see again Kahuku Point and Waianai as the trade wind piles up huge combers off the Hawaii coast. *Xiphias gladius* takes the bait tossed out to him and away he goes like a speedboat. Then, up he comes, leaping high and crashing down in a rain-bow of spray. Or, at Andros Island, in the balmy breezes of the Bahamas, I see *Galeocerdo tigrinus*, the tiger, make wide foamy circles about the boat while the leather harness creaks and this big hickory bends like a willow wand.

These rods stand, like others in the rack, as symbols of sport—as reminders of games we have played together—as beacons of hope that, God willing, we will play again. Each represents its own kind of angling, most of them different, but who can say which is the best? For me, each in its turn was the best.

The Call of the Sea

A lameness which I brought home with me from the World War put an end to my hunting and to my fishing on foot, but there had to be outlet for the sporting instinct developed in me by a life of service in the army with hunting and fishing around the world. Bass-fishing and blue-fishing were still practicable and I enjoyed them but, in Hawaii and the East, I had had a taste, a good big taste, of angling for heavy sea fish and this had somewhat marred my zest for pursuit of smaller varieties. Pegging away to find what I could do, I soon learned that though my stream-wading days were done, I could still be "Hell in the Swivel Chair!"

For many years I had had fun fishing in various ways for sharks, but now I took to angling for them with rod and reel at times when I could not reach other big fish and, in so doing, I developed for myself the somewhat unique or at least unusual game which I am about to describe. In pursuit of this I found new zest in combats with savage monsters to be conquered with ethical tackle and by match-ing one's brains against their strength.

[9]

Now, too, a new interest was added to the sport when I came to know Ulric Dahlgren, Professor of Biology at Princeton University, for that keen sportsman and splendid companion on some of my expeditions made shark-hunting take on somewhat the nature of scientific research. Later I came to know Doctor E. W. Gudger of the American Museum of Natural History who also helped guide my sport-fishing along scientific lines and I found that my sport had become a study.

Let me say here to other sportsmen that this was not drudgery and that without such interest he will miss a large part of the pleasure of his sport. Streams and sea are so full of strange creatures that one never ceases to find interesting species, and even the commonest varieties are well worth examination and study. Scientists of our great museums are searching for information which an amateur might help them find, and the amateur himself may get as much pleasure from a pickled specimen as from a fried fish.

It may fairly be inferred that shark-fishing is a vigorous sport but, paradoxical though it may seem, a man, even past middle age, in fair physical condition is not debarred from it for, to a certain extent, the angler controls the fight and so controls the energy used. He may "horse" the fish and thus bring about a tug-of-war which neither he nor his tackle could stand or, by taking advantage of opportunities, he can save his tackle and his strength, while the fish exhausts himself. The old hand at the game will "bring his shark to iron" without turning a hair though the athlete tyro, with the same shark, would have lost his fish and would be lying in the cockpit— played out. Yet I would not argue that a doctor (and, by the way, did you ever notice how many of them are sportsmen?) should prescribe shark-fishing as a rest cure.

ON ROD AND REEL

Recently a sportsman friend, nearly as old as I, wrote to me advising that I "go easy" and take up some lighter kind of fishing. I replied:

THE SWIVEL CHAIR

I used to chase the sporty trout with lurid gaudy fly
And follow him across the stream, on quicksand or on dry,
But, now, I cannot jump around, on rocks both slick and bare,
And, yet, out on the briny deep, I'm hell in the swivel chair.

Bass fishing was a lovely sport, in light and frail canoe
To balance which, though practical, was rather hard to do.
But this game now has also passed and gone beyond my flair
Though I am happy yet because I'm hell in the swivel chair.

If I tried now to stand up straight and cast a silken line,
'Twould wrap about companions' necks, as well as over mine.
I've got to quit these sporty games and yet I do not care
So long, as on the ocean swell, I'm hell in the swivel chair.

Now, you, Old Sport, who have to quit the games of yesteryear,
Can still find sport which ought to be quite every bit as dear.
If you can't wade and climb and jump, because of life's hard wear,
Content yourself with rod and reel—Be hell in the swivel chair.

Don't lie around on parlor couch nor mope on garden bench—
That only makes the muscles soft and gives the heart a wrench.
Get out your rod and bait your hook, in brilliant sunshine glare—
And fight pelagic monsters—Be hell in the swivel chair!

Now, there is encouragement for old sports—young ones should need no encouragement.

CAST OUT!

[11]

VITALITY AND POWER

RECONSTRUCTED JAW
Carcharodon megalodon

CHAPTER II

SHARKS IN GENERAL
PHYSICAL STRUCTURE—ORDER AND SPECIES

THE shark, belonging to one of the largest and commonest orders of fishes of the present times, is also one of the oldest living vertebrates. He has come down from past geological ages little changed except in size, for, big though he now is, he was larger then, fossil remains showing that he may have been over a hundred feet in length.

One almost needs logarithms to calculate the weight of such a fish but, since his length, exclusive of caudal fin, would be about 974 inches and his girth about 450 inches, his weight, by a rather reliable formula, would be:

$$\frac{\overline{450}^2 \times 974}{800} = 246543 \text{ lbs.—or about } 123 \text{ tons.}$$

Such conjectures aside, there is in the American Museum of Natural History the reconstructed jaw of one of the leviathans which swam the seas when glaciers covered the northern part of our continent. The fossil teeth of this *Carcharodon*, averaging 4¼ inches in length, found in the Tertiary deposits of North Carolina, are set in a jaw modelled after the jaw of the White Shark, his nearest living relative. This jaw would easily take in a four-poster bed and, from the estimated length of the fish, we can calculate his weight as over thirty-eight tons.

It may therefore be safely assumed that this shark was not caught on rod and reel or, if three hundred million years ago men did fish in that sporty way their fisherman's prayer was answered:

Lord grant to me to catch a fish
So big that even I
In talking of it to my friends
May never need to lie!

The shark is a true fish, not a mammal, though the fact that many species are viviparous has led to some popular confusion on this point.

Jordan and Evermann[1] catalog sharks, with skates and rays, in sub-class "Selachii" of the "Elasmobranchii," and in the "Asterospondyli" (Typical Sharks) of this sub-class are found most of the living species. These are characterized by five lateral gill-openings, two dorsal fins (without spines) and an anal fin. In these "true sharks," the lower jaw is not articulated with the skull which is of one piece of stiff cartilage, without sutures.

In his physical structure, the shark is highly specialized to meet conditions under which he exists, while, as a vital organism, he presents some features which are almost unique. Conspicuous among these are his spiral valvular digestive tract and his dual organs of reproduction. For a fish, he has a well-developed brain, his sense of smell is acute and his hearing is supplemented by nerves, which are extremely sensitive to vibration.

There is no air-bladder, as there is in most fishes, so the shark, deprived of this means of changing his specific gravity, must regulate his depth by swimming; he is therefore rarely seen quiescent.

1. *Fish of North and Middle America*, U. S. Natnl. Museum, Bulletin 46, 1896.

In nearly all species of true sharks, a long, lithe, muscular, fusi-form body tapers from its largest part, about a third of its length back of the nose, forward into a pointed conical head and aft into a long, round, graceful tail or peduncle, which terminates in a large swallow-tailed caudal fin, or fluke.

Different from the swimming of most fishes and characteristic of that of the shark are the sinuous undulations of his body by which he supplements caudal-fin propulsion and this gives to him a peculiar slithering, ghost-like glide. His litheness is in large part due to the absence from his body of stiff bones, for his frame is mainly of heavy cartilage; his only fossil remains are the enamel covered teeth.

Over his cartilaginous framework is stretched his truly marvel-ous muscular system covered by a denticled hide, so tough and so protected by small, close set, horny scales as to defy all but sharp, well tempered instruments and almost to justify the saying that "only a shark can bite a shark."

The first dorsal fin, usually large and erect, is much larger than the second dorsal, the anal and the ventrals. Pectorals are usually long and sickle-shape. The size, shape, and position of all of these fins vary with different species and are to be noted as important clues to identification. Only the caudal fin, which is also important for identification, is important in propulsion, other fins being used mainly for balancing and guiding.

Near the ventral fins, in male sharks, are found the claspers, which might be mistaken for fins but which in fact are sexual organs.

Gill-openings are usually five (in some species, seven) parallel vertical slits which are not covered as in other fishes, and the spacing of these slits is another clue for species identification.

[15]

The mouth, situated beneath the head, the nose projecting well beyond it, gives to the shark the familiar "overshot" disagreeable expression. The mouth is of enormous size and is sometimes supplied with as many as seven visible, parallel, curved rows of teeth. Only the forward of these rows are functional, those in the rear being in successive stages of development and inclination backward while still more rows have not made their appearance. The teeth are not set in the bone of the jaw but grow from a hardened skin of the mouth. As this skin grows forward the teeth develop and rise to vertical position and the rows are successively shed over the front edge of the mouth. The fish is thus constantly provided with new dentition and this explains why so many shark teeth are found on the shore and why fossil teeth are so abundant. The difference between teeth of species is a valuable means of identification as well as evidence of the habits of sharks of each species.

Most sharks either bite and swallow their food down large gullets, as do the White, the Blue and the Mackerel, or they crush it as do mollusk-eaters, like the Nurse and the Dogfish—none of them chew and masticate. Some species, notably the great Whale Shark, feed on small fishes, jellyfishes, small crustaceans and algae which pass down their small throats after being strained from huge volumes of water by their gill-brushes. For obvious reasons, their teeth are small, and one family, the Basker, substitutes for teeth a brush-like apparatus which serves as a sieve.

Even in the group which we may call "biting swallowers" there are different tooth shapes for the different species and this helps distinguish them. The Mackerel Shark has long pointed teeth, the White has broadly triangular ones, the Hammerhead combines these puncturing and cutting qualities in his narrow triangular teeth and

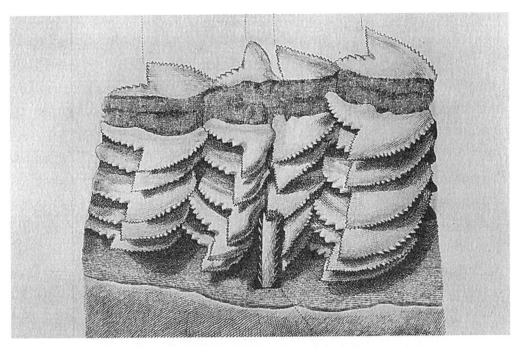

SECTION OF JAW OF TIGER SHARK

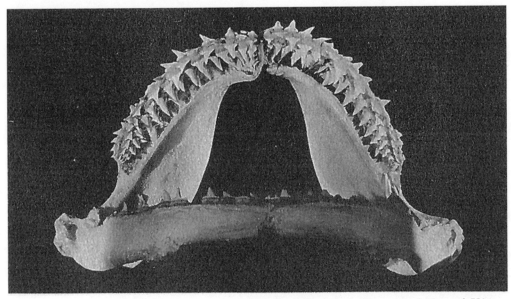

Courtesy of American Museum of Natural History

LOWER JAW OF A BLACK-TIPPED SHARK

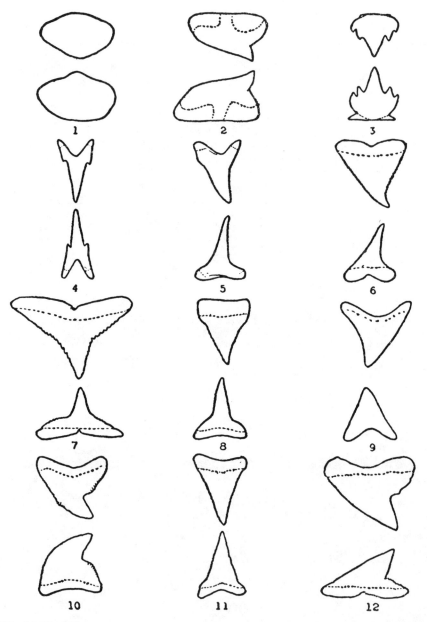

From "Shark! Shark!"　　　　　　　　　　　*Courtesy of Gotham House*

SHARK TEETH

An upper and lower tooth to the left of the symphysis: 1. Smooth Dog Shark. 2. Spined Dogfish. 3. Nurse Shark. 4. Sand Shark. 5. Mackerel Shark. 6. Blue Shark. 7. Spot-fin Ground Shark. 8. New York Ground Shark. 9. Thresher Shark. 10. Tiger Shark. 11. Man-eater Shark. 12. Hammer-head Shark.

the Tiger Shark's teeth are large, broad and sickle-shaped. The broad and rather flat teeth of mollusk-feeders are set like paving tiles and sometimes are practically joined together.

Fast swimming species feed usually on live fish which they pursue and capture, but slower ones may have to content themselves with mollusks, crustaceans or even with offal. In general, however, the shark is not a carrion feeder.

Most sharks are drab-colored creatures—dull blue, ashy grey, brownish or of some other inconspicuous tint. The small Tiger Shark of Ceylon, brilliant yellow and black, is one of the few sharks that is really gaudy though the great Whale Shark, the largest fish of modern times, is ornately decorated with a checkerboard of white and yellowish lines in the squares of which are brilliant yellow spots.

Breeding

Sharks are viviparous, oviparous and ovoviviparous. Those which we are especially considering in this book are all viviparous, some of them bearing as many as fifty pups each year. It is fortunate for the shark species that the females are so prolific for otherwise the high mortality of the young, sacrificed to the appetite of the older sharks, might soon result in extermination.

Oviparous sharks are in general even more prolific than viviparous species but much less so than most other fishes. Their eggs, however, are supplied with large yolks which serve to nourish the young fish until they can care for themselves. The young of the viviparous, developing within the mother, are nourished directly from her and are quite self-reliant at birth. In all species, therefore, mortality of young sharks is small as compared with other fishes.

[17]

Apparently, nature did not provide the young sharks primarily as food for other creatures as she seems to have done with some other fishes and she has given the hatchlings a generous emergency ration of egg yolk to carry them through a critical period. Other fishes are not so lavishly provided for.

The female cod, for example, lays as many as nine million eggs each year but only about one in two million of these becomes a mature reproducing fish. The herring lays about twenty-five thousand eggs of which less than one in ten thousand reaches maturity. Besides those which die of what we might call natural causes, other countless billions are eaten by fish, by birds and by animals all of which prey upon them from the time the egg is laid. Huxley estimates that but 5% of the herrings destroyed are victims of man and that 95% fall to other enemies. It is safe to say that sharks get their full share. It is perhaps fortunate for man that infant mortality is so high among fishes, for otherwise we might not be able to sail a boat on the ocean which would be a sort of fish chowder. What a premium one would have to pay on a life insurance policy for a juvenile fish!

ORDER AND SPECIES

In the sub-order of true sharks, there are at least fourteen families and there is a considerable number of kinds in each of these, making in all about a hundred and fifty species. Fortunately, there is no advantage to the sportsman in knowing all of these species for most of them never, or rarely, come to our waters. Yet, some of them which do not belong there are occasionally encountered, for the shark is a cruiser, a rover, and considerable of a vagabond.

The migrations of sharks are none too well understood but if by "migration" is meant the seasonal movement of great numbers of sharks, then they do migrate. Such changes of habitat do not seem to be for breeding, as in the case of salmon, nor are they concerted travels of a school, as with the bluefish. Rather are they the movements of great numbers of individuals at about the same time, probably following their migrating prey. So, for example, we find on the New Jersey coast, sharks are most numerous during the late summer when the great run of bluefish is at its height while in winter they are scarce.

In southern waters, where the abundance of food is less variable, the shark population is more constant but there, too, it depends largely upon the movements of other fishes and, even in the Bahamas, sharks are not abundant during the stormy season since sharks might well wish to avoid a Bahama hurricane even though food did not lure them elsewhere.

It is beyond my purpose to discuss all sharks which may be common to our waters, and I intend to dwell upon only a few of them which may give good sport on rod and reel. So, there are eliminated the little Dog Sharks, which rarely exceed three or four feet in length; Sand Sharks which, in spite of their size, are usually too logy to furnish good sport; and most of the Ground Sharks, which do not provide good angling. Also, the Thresher Shark, rarely taken on hook and line; the big Basking Shark, a northern form seen only occasionally in our waters, and the Nurse Shark which, though common along the Florida Cays, is not to be considered a sport-fish.

Certain Ground Sharks, notably the Spotted Fin, six feet long; the Southern Ground Shark, ten feet; and the New York Ground Shark, eight feet, are common and might be worthy of attention but none of them are to be compared, as game fighters, with pelagic, surface-swimming, live-fish-feeders, such as the White and the Mackerel Sharks.[2]

2. To spare the casual reader scientific classifications and descriptions and, nevertheless, to aid the angler, who may be so inclined, to identify his catch, an appendix follows, in which are briefly treated some of our common species; and let me say here that the angler who goes in for this exciting sport will greatly increase his pleasure by a knowledge of the quarry and also that his luck will be in direct proportion to his understanding of the characteristics and habits of the fish.

CHAPTER III

SHARK NATURE
CHARACTERISTICS AND HABITS

ANTHROPOPHAGY

A QUESTION sure to be asked when sharks are mentioned is: "Do sharks attack and kill men?" Whatever be the reply, there is likely to be a dispute, because the question, in such simple form, cannot be definitely and authoritatively answered.

Sharks do not go forth to stalk men as cats do mice nor to catch them as wolves do deer. Fish are the regular victims of even the most predatory sharks, and man, though probably an acceptable morsel, would be a most unexpected addition to their menus. Nevertheless, sharks do occasionally get him.

We can only guess at how much truth there may be in the yarns we hear of shark attacks, but there must be a more solid foundation than superstition and imagination for the general and real fear of sharks shared by practically all watermen, though few of them can cite cases of shark attacks within their own personal knowledge.

There are countless instances of the eating of dead men by sharks, and there are many reports of their attacks upon live men. Both our War Department and our Navy Department officially report several such killings. Governor Pinchot tells of one such in Tahiti, and Captain William Young has collected in his book some authentic reports. Nevertheless, I have repeatedly seen soldiers from transports, in shark-infested waters, swimming unharmed about the ship and thousands of tourists watch natives diving for pennies at tropical ports, where harbors are teeming with sharks, without ever seeing a diver harmed by one.

Probably the most dangerous species in our North Atlantic are the Great White Shark, the Great Blue Shark, and the Tiger Shark, none of which is really common in our waters, but it seems to be a generally accepted fact that sharks are more dangerous in the tropics where, incidentally, these species are more common.

To get facts in this much contended question of shark attacks on man, Mr. Herman Oelrichs, some years ago, offered, through New York papers, a reward of five hundred dollars for authentic information of such an attack in our waters, but the reward was never claimed. Similar rewards were later offered, and a number of papers took up the discussion which brought to light no credible instance in our zone though there were a number in tropic waters.[1]

The late Dr. F. A. Lucas, of the American Museum of Natural History, quite thoroughly investigated this subject and he believed that the danger of being attacked by a shark in the vicinity of New York is "infinitely less than that of being struck by lightning." Nevertheless, periodic shark scares persist, and in one of these, in 1932, newspapers published alarming casualties from our bathing beaches. Some resorts even safeguarded swimmers by wire fences in the surf and the barbs of these were probably more dangerous to the bathers than were the teeth of sharks.

At the height of this excitement Mr. C. M. Breder, Jr., of the New York Aquarium, made a trip to study conditions in local waters, but found sharks no more numerous nor ferocious than usual and he concluded that most of the panic was probably due to publicity and

1. Brooklyn Museum Bulletin, Vol. 3, No. 1.

exaggeration and that at that time there was not an authentic case of attack by sharks in our region. It is quite necessary to realize that there is a difference between shark bite and shark attack and that lack of caution may, and often does, result in severe laceration from the teeth or in a terrific wallop from the tail of a frightened or wounded shark.

In some parts of the world sharks are much more dangerous than they are with us and Dr. C. H. Townsend, Director of the New York Aquarium, has furnished an article[2] which should remove all skepticism as to whether sharks will attack men. He cites numerous instances in which men were attacked and devoured and tells of cases where not only were swimming men seized but also where sharks grabbed the oars or outriggers of boats.

In Polynesia, the almost amphibious natives regard the shark with a dread akin to that of the African for the lion, though the shark takes less toll in human life because he cannot stalk his prey, as does the lion, on land.

In Australia, the shark is a greater danger than he is with us. Especially is he a menace in Sydney Harbor where his predatory habits have doubtless been encouraged by the custom of disposing of slaughterhouse refuse in the bay and so chumming up the sharks.

In the Solomon Islands, sharks are singularly bold and ferocious, which may be accounted for by the custom of disposing of the dead by throwing their bodies into the sea—thus literally training the sharks to eat men.

Interesting conclusions of Dr. Townsend are that sharks of tropical waters are more ferocious than those of temperate zones, that sharks are more dangerous at night than in day, and that the

2. Bulletin 34, N. Y. Zool. Society, Vol. XXXIV, No. 6, 1931.

most dangerous time is dusk. Also he believes that large sharks are not necessarily more dangerous than those not so large and that all sharks are particularly dangerous when swarming on feeding grounds.

This all seems to confirm my own belief that, while sharks do not set out on man-hunts, they will, under favorable circumstances, attack man, especially if impelled by hunger, excitement or the blood-scent, and that they are particularly dangerous when in feeding swarms.

It is going a little strong to say, as recently did one scientist, that a shark will not attack man unless he gets the blood-scent for, though that unquestionably excites him, there are many authentic cases where he has attacked without it. Nevertheless, it is my opinion that a shark, except when surprised, attacked or greatly excited, rarely attacks a man whom he does not believe to be dead or helpless; and I believe that, except in self-defense, a shark prefers to avoid anything which might fight back. It is prudent, however, not to risk being the victim in an exceptional case. Since the angler, if he accepts my advice, will try to stay in his fair-sized motorboat, the man-eating tendencies of sharks are not of immediate importance, nor is it here necessary to convict or acquit the shark of anthropophagy. Suffice it to say that I do not recommend him as playmate at a bathing beach.

IGNORANCE AND HATRED OF SHARKS

A serious charge against the shark and one which can be sustained, is the great damage he does to fish-traps and nets, and the tremendous toll he takes of fish which men want for themselves.

This indictment of the shark may serve to salve the conscience of the sportsman who goes forth to assassinate him. Certainly it will make easier the getting of bait because seinemen are ever ready to contribute trash fish for a fight against their archenemy.

It is remarkable how little is known of the habits and characteristics of this oldest and largest of our common fishes. Even Garman, the recognized authority on shark taxonomy, barely touches upon this subject. Sharks have swum the waters of our globe for more than three hundred million years but much about them still remains a mystery. Let a man embark upon an investigation of them and he will soon find himself engulfed in such a welter of scientific fact, unsubstantiated legend, imaginative folklore and plain garden variety of fish story, that he is hopelessly swamped. He will probably conclude that he is dealing with "all kinds of a fish" as, in fact, he is, for the order, Plagiostomia, includes the huge Manta and the little Skate, the great Whale Shark and the small Dogfish, the vicious White Shark and the cowardly Nurse. There are among the sharks deep-sea flesh-eaters and shoal water mollusk-feeders. They are found beneath Arctic ice and on tropic coral reefs. They cruise mid-ocean and haunt the waters of coastal marshes, but, wherever sharks may be, they are undisputed masters, and upon their slithering approach all other denizens fin away. Whether harmless to man or a menace to him, they are hideous and they are hated.

There may be justification for this hatred of the savage predatory shark and for the descriptive "hideous," usually applied to him, but in fact it is only his face, with leering sinister eyes and dreadful spiked teeth, which makes him hideous, otherwise his graceful form and delicate shade would make him beautiful. No creature of the sea is so gracefully lithe as the shark, silently gliding through the water, but none is so terribly fearsome as he when he dashes at his prey.

LIVES OF CRUEL CANNIBALS

With their equipment for offense and defense, sharks have naught to fear in the sea where no other fish will attack them, where their only danger is from other sharks, where their whole existence is but a continuous search for food to satisfy insatiable appetite. The shark is always hungry—he suffers from incurable bellyache. Be it live fish, dead fish, flesh or fowl, all is grist for the shark's mill and he is always on a predatory prowl after it. Never does he seem to rest. His big fins appear above the surface, or beneath it he slithers in from nowhere, but he is always headed for the same objective—food.

What may be the span of the natural life of a shark is yet undetermined for he has no scales, whose rings might tell his age, and his teeth are but temporary equipment. It is doubtful, however, whether many sharks live out their natural lives for, if ever they lose, even temporarily, the capacity to defend themselves, other sharks are quick to kill and eat them.

Sharks are the most cannibalistic of cannibals and in large ones are often found smaller ones which have been devoured. Doctor E. W. Gudger, of the American Museum of Natural History, has published a most thorough and instructive paper on shark cannibalism, in which he shows that practically all sharks prey upon other sharks as well as upon their cousins, the Skates and Rays.[3]

I once saw taken from the stomach of an eight-foot shark, a

3. Gudger, E. W., "Cannibalism among Sharks and Rays," *Science Monthly*, May, 1932.

three-footer which had been swallowed whole. To appreciate that gastronomic accomplishment, one must remember not only the size of the morsel but also the sharp teeth, the hard stiff fins, capable of cutting a heavy line, and the tough denticled hide which defies ordinary tanning processes. One wonders at gastric juices which can digest such things as are taken from the stomachs of sharks: for example, a horse's hoof with the iron shoe on it—the bones had been completely dissolved, the horn casing was softened to the consistency of leather and the iron was being rapidly corroded. Could doctors use shark juice instead of pig juice to get pepsin? In this digestive fluid there is a very high content of hydrochloric acid, and I have seen it remove the varnish when spilled on a deck.

Nevertheless, we read in Darwin's *Voyage of the Beagle*—"I have heard from Dr. Allan, of Forres, that he has frequently found a Diodon,[4] floating alive and distended in the stomach of a shark; and that on several occasions he has known it eat its way, not only through the coats of the stomach, but through the sides of the monster, which has thus been killed. Who would ever have imagined that a little soft fish could have destroyed the great savage shark?" —Who would imagine it? We must say, like Charles Dana, "Important if true," but we may conjecture at least that the Diodon had an uncomfortable swim.

It is not uncommon for sharks to attack another shark when he is held on a line and to bite great chunks out of him, and it is still more common to find sharks which have been partially devoured while they were enmeshed in nets. Apparently, they live in armed neutrality, but when one of them becomes disabled or helpless his comrades give him short shrift.

4. Species of *Puffer Fish*.

[27]

Speaking of the slashing of one shark by another brings to mind the old superstition that a shark must turn on his back or side to bite. To one who has watched sharks take the bait and who has seen them bite one another, this is of course utter nonsense. A shark's eyes are not well placed for forward-downward vision, so he may have to roll for better view; and, frequently, the roll is but the preliminary of his dash at an object.

Another foolish idea is that female sharks swallow their young to protect them, disgorging them when captured. The fact is that, on capture, viviparous females often give birth to their young and, incidentally, it may surprise you to see how self-reliantly the pups swim away when tossed overboard.

The shark's tenacity of life is amazing. He seems to be immune to nervous shock, cruel wounds affect him only slightly, and he remains dangerous a long time out of water. I have seen a shark, whose liver had been removed for chum, swim strongly away and I once saw a boatman knocked over the gunwale by a shark which had been in the boat nearly an hour.

Contrary to popular idea, the shark is wary, almost timid, for monster though he is, he is averse to taking chances. He is, however, possessed of a curiosity which sometimes urges him on and makes him appear bold when, in fact, he is terrified; but at heart, if his heart be aught but a blood-pump, he is an arrant coward.

Nothing could better illustrate the curiosity and the timidity of sharks than an incident related in Captain Young's book: A diver working with him in Hawaii was constantly surrounded by curious sharks which, however, did not molest him but, when they nosed up uncomfortably close, the diver released some air bubbles from his wrist-band and this sent them gliding away.

Even a large shark, with a large skull, has but a handful of brain-matter for the brain-cavity is only partly filled. Nevertheless, this handful seems to provide him with a disproportionate amount of suspicion and with perception enough to beware of a bait tied onto a string. I have seen sharks rush furiously up to a bait then stop, draw back and examine it, but they would instantly seize and gobble an identical free bait floated out to them.

For some inexplicable reason, sharks are particularly suspicious of dark objects while light-colored ones seem to attract them. They will take, as bait, a skinned fish in preference to a fish with dark hide and they seem to prefer whitish fish rather than dark ones. This is strange, because darkish Skates and Rays are their favorite natural food; these, however, are light underneath.

A striking example of the attractiveness of light objects to sharks is told by Captain William Young who says that one day when towing a dead black horse to attract sharks, a shark followed but would not come within harpoon range. When a newspaper was thrown overboard, however, its white flash caused the shark to dash up and he was harpooned.

Captain Young, in his wide experience with sharks, intimates also that this peculiarity makes the negroes of the West Indies more immune from shark attack than white men. He tells how native divers smear their white palms and soles with tar, but one scientist believes that the protection is due to the fact that sharks do not like the smell of tar and that even the smell of marlin will keep them from a bait. Quite opposed to this theory, Mr. Schuetz, Bahamas Manager of the National Fisheries Corporation, uses tar liberally on his equipment. The buoy and anchor lines of his nets are of steamed tarred rope, and bait is tied to the meshes with tarred marlin, all of which does not seem to discourage the sharks. On the other hand, Schuetz absolutely confirms the idea that sharks are attracted by light-colored objects and for that reason he has, after experiment, adopted white nets which he has found to be superior to those of the various colors tried, or to nets camouflaged to resemble the bottom. In my own experience, I have noticed no advantage in any color of line, white, green or natural.

I mention all this to show how different are the opinions as to the likes and dislikes of this fish.

Usually a shark does not take the bait with a rush but will first seize it in his teeth before swallowing it. When, however, he has decided, he takes it with a gulp.

However hesitant sharks may ordinarily be, all hesitation leaves them with the smell of fresh blood which puts them into a frenzy. Testing this one day when several sharks were cautiously nosing at my bait, I poured over the side of the boat some blood from a recently captured shark. Instantly one of the investigators seized the bait and the others went frantic. Taking advantage of this characteristic, I have always since then bled newly caught sharks over the gunwale, usually with good results.

Under skin-flaps in the anterior portion of a shark's head are two large nostrils and as his olfactory organs are excellent, his sense of smell is acute. He gets the blood-scent at amazing distances and rushes toward it. Literally, it seems to make him see red.

For this reason, blood is good chum and there is no better chum than the warm rich blood of the porpoise, though any blood, from fish, fowl or animal, will attract sharks.

When not excited by the blood-scent, sharks are surprisingly wary and alert. As they circle the boat, their unblinking yellow eyes are ever on watch, and their sensitive nerves are always atune. A wave of the hand or a sudden noise sends them gliding away, to return, probably, when impelled by irresistible curiosity or insatiable appetite.

By "noise," I mean vibration or jar in the water for I have observed that they do not seem to be afraid of other noises such as loud talking, for example. To try this out, I have even shouted at sharks swimming close to the boat without alarming them in the least, but a bang on the boat-bottom sent them dashing away. Nevertheless, for some unknown reason, talking seems to make them timid about taking the bait.

Most sharks are very moderately gregarious but, where one is found, there will probably be others, temporarily together, because their individual searches have led them to that place on the trail of food. When their maws are filled, or when the possibilities of the locality are exhausted, they will leave to resume their ceaseless prowls in search of more food.

In most sharks there is little instinct to school, like the Bluefish for example, though some of the smaller species do at times swarm, and Nurse Sharks and certain Sand Sharks assemble in great numbers in shallow water at breeding season.[5]

Being masters of the sea, sharks need not join for defense; community of interest does not exist in their selfish, individualistic natures, and, in their lives, every fish is for himself. Most animals and many fishes unite against common foes but sharks do not, unless there be prospect of a feast after the battle.

Even a ewe will fight for her offspring, but I have never heard

5. Mr. Schuetz believes that the Nurse Sharks which assemble in shallow water are mostly females resting there during a period of pregnancy.

[31]

of such action by a female shark. When her pups are born she is done with them.

In the study of animals, or even of fishes, a man usually finds something likable about them, but in the monstrous, cruel, cowardly shark he can find not one admirable trait—he is simply a tiger.

COMMERCIAL VALUE OF SHARKS

This large, ubiquitous and abundant fish which, except to a few sportsmen, has for centuries been but a nuisance, has recently become of economic value, and commercial companies are now engaging in shark-fishing as a profitable enterprise. Their catches, taken in large specially constructed nets, are measured by tons and practically all of this weight of fish is utilized. Formerly, shark hide or "shagreen" was used mainly as an abrasive, like sandpaper, and it was of great service for cleaning decks. Its non-slippery quality made it useful for sword hilts and tool handles and its durability for bags and pocketbooks; only recently a process of tanning was discovered which effectively and economically removes the denticles of the skin, and thus converts the hide into a beautiful leather of superior toughness and durability, called "galuchat."

The liver of a shark may be a fourth or a fifth of his weight and oil from the liver, about four gallons from a six-footer, is used in tempering steel, in paint, and in many other commercial ways. Medicinally, it has been found to possess vitamins which make it a rival of cod-liver oil.

Dried fins, used for the famous shark-fin soup, bring good prices wherever there is a Chinese population, and quantities of them are exported to China. This soup is made of the dried fins, is much like turtle soup and is delicious.

Courtesy of E. M. Schuetz

TIGERS

A HAUL OF THE NATIONAL FISHERIES CORPORATION

Tons of sharks ready for processing

Courtesy of E. M. Schuetz

BRINGING IN THE CATCH

Certain varieties of shark whose flesh is especially fine of texture and delicate of flavor, are marketed as "steak fish" and "grey fish," others are salted and packed, while plugs punched from shark steaks and ray fins and doped with clam juice, become "deep sea scallops." The less desirable flesh is dried and ground into poultry meal and the remainder is reduced to fertilizer.

The prejudice against eating shark meat seems largely due to the idea that sharks are scavengers as, in fact, some of them are, though no more so than most other fishes and crustaceans, especially crabs and lobsters; and I know of at least one famous trout pool which is close to a sewer outlet.

Many people enjoy shark meat without suspecting what they are eating. Once, while watching my boatman skin and trim a two hundred pounder, I asked, "What are you going to do with that shark?" Grinning, he replied, "This was shark—now it is just fish—tomorrow, in the market, it will be swordfish."

An enthusiastic tarpon angler once asked me, "Why do you fish for sharks? What good are they?" "What good are tarpon?" I replied. The answers to both of our questions could be, "The sport of catching them." We liberate the tarpon because they are such poor eating, and we kill the sharks because they are predatory nuisances. A shark who had read his Shakespeare might, paraphrasing, say, "As flies to wanton boys, are we to *men*. They kill us for their sport."

CATCHING SHARKS

Sharks may be caught on heavy cable hand-line, and it is lively work doing it; and I have caught them on a short chain suspended from a floating barrel which was followed until the shark exhausted himself trying to submerge it.

Once, in the Philippines, when our transport lay anchored at Mariveles Quarantine Station, at the entrance of Manila Harbor, some of us young officers, while waiting to learn whether or not we were going to come down with Asiatic cholera, employed our time in catching huge sharks which circled about the ship. The chief engineer had made for us a large hook on which, at the end of a stout rope, we got a lot of sharks, hoisting them aboard by snatch-block and winch. Some of these fish weighed more than a thousand pounds and the catching of them was great fun, though, perhaps, not ethical angling. They provided the chief engineer with a barrel of fine oil.

Both Havana Harbor and the Harbor of Santiago de Cuba swarm with sharks,—"Tiburones," the natives call them, and especially in Havana I had great sport, even though I had not then learned to use rod and reel for sharks.

Recently the newspapers reported that shark-fishing in Havana Harbor had been prohibited, ostensibly because human remains found in a shark were identified as those of an important political prisoner who had been confined in Cabañas Fortress. In Spanish days there were stories of a mysterious trap door in Cabañas, which overhangs the harbor. Perhaps Machado's government was still using this trap door and did not wish its mystery disclosed by sharks.

In Honolulu we towed a dead horse out into the bay and when sharks were following we used hand-line or harpoons.

Notwithstanding what I have said of the commercial value of sharks, there will be no economic return from those caught by the sportsman unless he happens to have a compost heap, and it is from the sportsman's viewpoint that we are considering this game. That eliminates nets and hand-lines and barrels, because the greatest sport will come with the rod and reel.

There is a glamour to this fishing which comes with no other angling. I have tried to analyze its fascination, which seems really to be the zest of combat with the "Tiger of the Sea," for whom there is no feeling of pity to mar the exultation of victory. Even for the swordfish, which may be as big and as strong as most sharks, one feels a regret when he is killed; but, for the shark, there is no compassion—he is a Pariah. When he is brought up, his glaring amber eyes evoke no feeling of kindliness and his snapping jaws, with dreadful dagger teeth, convey only the impression that he is an armed enemy who would give no quarter and who is entitled to none. From the moment when he takes the hook, his capture is a fight—a fight which excites the lust to kill a predatory creature whose life is a menace to all other denizens of the sea, and whose death will make the angler their protector.

The struggle between angler and shark is, however, like the taking of most game, a one-sided battle, for no man who is properly equipped and who knows his business can be in more than infinitesimal danger from a fish whose main purpose is to escape. I have caught many sharks but never have I seen one deliberately rush at a boat nor have I seen one try to capsize it or smash it with his tail, as they tell us in story books. It has been done, but it is not usual, and in all cases that I have been able to verify it was without success for the fish. If a man should put out his arm within reach of a frantic shark, he might have his hand amputated or, if he takes aboard an unexhausted shark, he may have his gunwale smashed or a plank knocked out; but such accidents would be due to his own stupidity. When a big shark is brought alongside, he should be given the harpoon and allowed to bleed out his energy at the end of its lanyard, jabbed with the killing-lance or swatted on the snout with a club.

[35]

By all this, I mean simply to emphasize that there is little danger in shark-fishing when it is done intelligently. But carelessness with a live shark is like monkeying with a buzz saw.

CHAPTER IV

SHARK-FISHING—EARLY EXPERIENCES
START OF ANGLING

MY first exciting experience with the shark was as a youngster in my early teens. I used to go out on Matompkin
Inlet, on the Atlantic side of the Eastern Shore of Virginia, with a crew of market fishermen. Those were wonderful days,
when glorious fishing always ended in a sailing race between the
fishing boats up Folly Creek to Drummondtown, each boat trying to
be first to market. One day, boylike, I had gotten into the dory
swinging astern of the "bateau" "Lottie Garrison" and was fishing
there when a big Hammerhead whizzed past, turned and began
slowly circling the boats. From my pocket I took a large hook which
I had treasured there for weeks, tied it onto the end of the painter of
the dory which was simply looped over a cleat on the "bateau." I
baited it with a weakfish and cast out. As it floated on the surface
fifty feet away, the Hammerhead on his next turn took it with a
gulp—"Snap!"—The painter tightened and the dory's bow went
almost underwater, bobbing up and down, while its stern skidded
crazily from side to side. I managed to whip the loop free from the
"bateau," scrambled over the thwarts to the stern of the dory, and
got an oar into the sculling groove. So, holding the dory head-on, I
was taken for a ride at speed hitherto never experienced by me in a
small boat, for motors had not then been invented. "Where the hell
do you think you're going?" shouted Captain Billy Milner, as I
scudded past. This was really a useless question, for no one could

have had less idea than I had of where I was going. I was on my way, however, and I was going fast.

I seem still to hear the unparliamentary remarks shouted after me by that salty crew whose fishing I was spoiling at the very best of the tide, for Captain Billy, who felt some responsibility for me, had ordered fishing lines in and sails up. Overboard went his cable and he was after us, but we had a half-mile start before, leaning to the breeze, the "bateau" was under headway. In a mile or so they had nearly overhauled us but my tug then suddenly changed its mind and we shot off to windward, giving our pursuers a two-mile beat of it before Captain Billy grabbed the dory's stern with a boat-hook and his crew dropped sails. Then shark, dory and "bateau" moved in procession at a somewhat slower speed until strong arms hauled in the offending shark and murdered him. By this time the crew, in the excitement of the chase, was no longer murderous in its intentions toward me and I was thrilling with delight at the sport I had given them, quite unpenitent of having spoiled their morning's catch. On the contrary, I think I was proud of having provided such an incident. From that time on I have been a confirmed shark-fisher, but I was too closely watched by Billy ever again to play that game when out with him.

This shark had every temptation to attack the little dory, but he did not do it, nor since then, under similar circumstances, have I seen one do it.

On one occasion in the Philippines I was shark-fishing from a canoe. A big Tiburone was towing us around, when he suddenly turned and rushed head-on against the boat. His impact threw the two paddlers and me into the bottom and, as I wallowed there, I had a distinct sense of relief when I felt the rope tauten as the shark, having swung away, took up the slack. This might make a fine story of a shark attack, but I am afraid that I will have to admit that the shark had no intention of attacking that boat but simply collided with it in his frantic efforts to escape.

In both of these experiences, I was using a hand-line which was my principal method of shark-fishing for many years and with it I had lots of fun. For hand-line fishing, my tackle was twenty fathoms of quarter-inch Manila rope and a dog chain to which was attached the hook, made by a local blacksmith. I had developed a technique which was to drive the hook into the shark's mouth by a heavy tug on the line and then to throw a turn around a cleat.

A strong man, much more a small boy, will have difficulty in hauling in a medium-sized shark, but I always got him in by taking up slack when his gyrations permitted and holding my gains by a turn around a cleat.

Sometimes I would tie my line to the painter and allow the shark to tow the boat. That added to the pleasure of a boat ride the thrill of the risk of capsizing, of being grounded on an oyster-bed or of being dragged among pound-net-poles—All excitements which were fascinating to a boy!

One day I was out anchored in a sailing skiff and had, as usual, put over my shark-line which was promptly seized by a fair-sized Sand Shark. This fellow simply went away to the end of the rope and there he sounded.

After a long wait, during which the shark showed no inclination to change his tactics, a passing skiff, carrying out seinemen, answered my hail. "What's the matter, youngster?" called the helmsman, running close. "I've got a shark!" I triumphantly trumpeted through my hands. "Well I'll be damned! Keep him!" the voice

[39]

boomed back with a chorus of guffaws. "But, Sir, won't you fellows help me land him?" But he was salty and adamant: "You want us to help haul in a shark, eh? Well, we've got nets to haul and we haven't lost no sharks, either. Cut 'im loose, boy!" and the skiff foamed past.

There were serious objections to cutting that shark loose. In the first place, I wished to catch him, and also my rope, dog chain and hook had cost real money; so, astride the tiller, I made my plans and then I hoisted anchor, broke out sail and, in spite of the shark, did not capsize. With the shark's obstreperous actions, handling the skiff was ticklish business but I beat and reached and ran for several hours until he was about drowned to docility. Then I essayed entrance into the creek where I presented my prize to a farmer. He consigned him to the compost pile, where His Sharkship "suffered a land change into something rich and strange" and he was probably sold the following year in the Baltimore markets as potatoes and tomatoes.

The white fishermen of the "Eastern Shore" detest sharks because of the loss they suffer from them, but, to this detestation, the colored population add a superstitious dread. Of the colored men about the place, Silas, alone, was ever ready to go fishing with me and I always wanted him because he saved me the labor of stepping masts and hoisting anchor. One day we took with us Tom, a young man who affected to share the contempt which Silas had for sharks, and who kept repeating Silas' slogan: "Dey kaint hurt yer in de boat."

We were soon hung onto a big shark which they were hauling in while I, at the tiller, maneuvered the skiff to give them slack. In process of these operations, the shark swished the rope across the stern, and, catching Tom's leg, threw him overboard. He could swim, and all he had to do was to get hold of the rope and haul aboard by it but the idea of a shark at the other end of that rope, fifty yards away, was so horrible that Tom was deprived of reason and, his eyes rolling white while the tide took him back, he simply howled: "Bring dat boat! O Lord, get dat shark outen here! O Lord, take dat shark away!"

When we finally hauled Tom (and the shark) aboard, Tom was given the honor of being allowed to bash in the shark's head with a hatchet. At the first wallop, the shark opened and snapped his jaws. "Shut yer mouf, Shark!" yelled Tom, with another wallop, "I'se seed all I wants ter see of dem teeths—an' I'se done felt 'em too—tearin' through my gizzard when I was back thar in de water wid yer!"

It is not only our colored people who hold sharks in such dread. I remember that once, when some of us young officers were shark-fishing at Havana, we noticed the native boatman crossing himself whenever we hooked a shark. At first we thought he was expressing to his patron saint appreciation of our good luck, but later we learned that he was beseeching protection from the danger to which the reckless young Americanos were exposing him.

In a Dory—A Mackerel Shark on a Rod

I had had great fun in Cuba, in Hawaii and in the Philippines with sharks, so when I came home to Virginia, in the early nineteen hundreds, I persisted in the sport of my boyhood there and usually kept most of the boats at my father's place, at Cape Charles, smeared with evil smelling shark blood. I was still using hand-lines, harpoons and barrels, but had never attempted to catch big sharks on rod and reel.

Throughout my fishing career, I had been pestered by sharks—Dog Sharks, Bonnetheads, Hammerheads, Mackerel Sharks, Sand Sharks, and Duskies. Little sharks and big sharks had snapped my lines, kinked my rods and slashed fine fish which I was bringing up; but never, until one day at the Virginia Capes, had I realized what sport there might be in catching these pests on ethical tackle. "Sharks! Sport-fish on rod and reel! You're crazy!" would have been my reaction to such an idea.

That day, I had a fine forty-pound Drumfish right up for the gaff when a glint of grey in a swirl of foam flashed at the boatside and when it disappeared so did half of my Drum.

"George," said I to the boatman, "if these darned things are after a game, let's play with 'em." Making a leader of a handy piece of bale wire and putting on a big hook, I baited it with the half drum left me and tossed out.

Immediately the bait was seized and the reel shrieked. Novice though I then was in shark taxonomy, I recognized the sharp snout, robust streamline body and keel-like side ridges of a Mackerel Shark, probably the fastest and gamest of our Atlantic species.

Realizing that my channel-bass tackle was not equal to a fight from an anchored sloop, such as this promised to be, and knowing that we could not up-anchor before the fish reached the end of my twelve-strand line, I jumped into the dory's bow and George, following me, threw off the painter and seized the oars.

All reel drags were squeezed hard down and I was pressing the thumb-pad except when I had to slip line to spare it more than test strain yet half of the three hundred yards were out and the line hummed like a telegraph wire before we had the boat under way. "Faster! Faster! Follow him! Follow him!" I urged the sweating

YOU CAN'T STOP HIM!

YOU MUST PUMP HIM UP

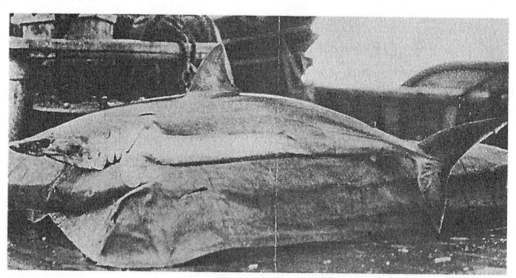

From Copeia   *Courtesy of American Society of Ichthyologists*

A MACKEREL SHARK
Isurus tigris

George who was then doing his very best but the reel spindle was already showing in spots when we began to hold our own.

After two miles of this chase, during which I had alternately slipped and recovered line, we began to gain a little on the fish and we were obliquing off to try to get a sideways pull to turn him.

We were then out beyond the point where John Smith landed, and we knew no more than he when he set out where we were headed for. With numb hands and aching back I held hard while George set an example for a Henley champion. In another mile, we were almost abreast of the tiring shark who now began to yield to my "pumping" and was turning. A little more and we had him circling the boat, a hundred yards off, so we on an inner circle could keep abreast of him. Around and around, seventeen times, he went, his sharp fin and crescent fluke showing above his white surge and then, off he went in another straight-away rush which took out most of my laboriously recovered line and scorched the thumb-pad. Then, suddenly ceasing his rush, he sounded to the bottom and we rowed up directly over him. In spite of hard pumping he could not be budged. He might as well have been the anchor until I chanced to remember an old trick.

Taking a bait "jimmy-crab," I locked his claws to encircle my line and let him slide down. Hardly had his wiggling legs landed on the shark's nose when up came the shark and off he went like a dog with a can to his tail. He was simply wild. Never had I seen such speed in a fish! It was one of the few times I had seen a shark leap clear of the water but up he went, once, twice, three times, like a tarpon, and, by these gyrations, he threw the crab. Then he settled down to more circling on the surface but he never again sounded. The "jimmy-crab" had cured him of that!

[43]

No living creature could expend such energy without tiring so, in two hours, he was thoroughly exhausted. I was tired, too, and George slumped over his oars. Finally, the double line came up, followed by the leader and George led the shark to the gunwale, now only waving his tail but still vicious enough to grind his lance-like teeth on the boat's planking. The gaff struck into the vital gills but, made for a seventy-five pound Channel Bass, its crook straightened under the weight of this big fish who in his frantic threshing deluged us with bloody spray and sank to be pumped up again. This time we got a slip-knot over his tail and hauled him aboard. A beautiful specimen of Mackerel Shark weighing more than two hundred pounds. What a fish! I have caught many bigger sharks but never a gamer one!

"George," I shouted, "what do you think of it?" "Well, suh," he replied, mopping his face with a scrub-rag, "I thinks I prefers drum-fishin'."

Perhaps the sweat in George's eyes had kept him from seeing the possibilities in the new sport which I had discovered at our very door, and in which we could indulge when tuna and other big fish were not accessible. I saw those possibilities, however, and I began experimenting with tackle and bait, and hunting for the places where sharks were most likely to be found. The hydrographic charts on my father's study walls were no longer used by me for navigation but for locating the tide runs where sharks would be looking for prey.

While I was probably the first to take up the sport of angling for sharks in that vicinity, I was by no means the first shark fisherman in the Chesapeake and we must give the credit for that to John Smith who came there some years ago and who nearly met his death

[44]

by trying to spear a Selachian with his rapier, not ethical tackle, by the way. The place where he got a stingray spike through his thigh is still known as Stingaree Point.

CHAPTER V

SHARK-FISHING ON THE ATLANTIC COAST

ALL along our Atlantic Coast, offshore and in bays, there is good shark-fishing and it is surprising how few anglers avail themselves of it. Do they think that it is as uncertain and as expensive as sword-fishing or do they say, as I used to say: "Sharks!—You're crazy!"

Inside there are probably more sharks, but outside on the open sea, the pelagic species are likely to be larger and gamer. I have had good sport at the Virginia Capes, which are taken here as a typical locality, but let me say that neither there nor anywhere else can we be sure that great numbers will always be caught.

Sharks, though numerous, are quite as uncertain in their movements as most fishes. In fact, their movements seem to be determined by those of other fish. When, for instance, schools of bluefish and mackerel are abundant many sharks will probably be following them, but when the schools go elsewhere, the sharks, too, are likely to go.

This suggests the rather obvious remark that when you are out after sharks you must hunt them. Watch for shark fins, watch for other fish breaking at the surface, and follow flocks of circling gulls feeding on fish scraps which rise where sharks are tearing schools to pieces.

At the Virginia Capes

From Cape Charles northward, a string of low islands (Fisherman's, Smith's, Cobb's, etc.), stretching between the open sea and the mainland, makes a narrow sound—the "River," it is locally called —which opens into the ocean through inlets between the islands.

The comparatively quiet water of the "River," bordered by wide marshes with deep tide channels, teems with marine life and is, therefore, an ideal feeding ground for small and medium-sized sharks, while larger ones hang around outside the inlets waiting for rejects from seines and traps or for other food to drift out with the ebb tide.

In some degree, therefore, an angler may choose whether, by staying inside, he will have several fights with sharks of from fifty to a hundred and fifty pounds, or whether he will go outside and try for a big fellow which might weigh a thousand.

With but slight knowledge of his country's history and with but little imagination, no American could be bored while waiting for fish at the Virginia Capes.

Had he been fishing these historic waters some three hundred and thirty years ago, his chum-streak would have been cut by prows of ships bearing the first English settlers to the New World. Here, as well, he could have hailed that doughty explorer, John Smith, and joined him in an oyster lunch ashore with "The Laughing King of Accawmacke." What fish stories John could have told, for he was himself something of a two-handed romancer!

A hundred and seventy-five years later, his fishing would have been spoiled by the detonations of the guns of the French and British fleets which decided here the fate of Cornwallis at Yorktown.

Through these Capes, entered the "Monitor" to give battle to the "Merrimac," and here was heard the firing of that first fight between iron-clads, that fight which changed all naval warfare.

Battleships and transports of the Civil War here passed continuously in and out; American troops sailed from here to Cuba and from here to France.

The history of our country constantly carries us back to these waters where so much of it has been made, since the day John Smith sailed in through these Capes to the day our troops sailed out through them for the World War. With the coming of the white man, the country about these waters became a battleground; and there man has ever since continued to struggle. Fringing these waters, the forests which echoed the twang of Indian bowstring and the crack of settler's rifle, reverberated, in later wars, with the boom of big guns and the crash of bursting shells. Such musing might well cause the angler to miss his bites, but he could not overlook the strike of a shark.

BOAT AND EQUIPMENT

Inside, the angler will probably find that an ordinary fishing boat and regular light tuna tackle will suffice, but outside, he should be equipped for heavy deep-sea fishing.

His boat, large enough for considerable sea, must be fast enough to follow the rushes of the fish and handy enough to maneuver with them.

The boatman, no less than the angler, must understand the game and from his wheel, in sight of the rod-man, he must conform the movements of the boat to those of the fish.

I like the swivel chair in the cockpit, aft of midships, from which position the fish can be fought always over the side rather than over pitching bow or whirring propeller and, throughout the struggle, the boat should be kept broadside on to the fish, not only so the line may not foul deckhouse, flagstaff or tiller but also because it will be in better position to conform to the movements of the fish.

The angler should be in a swivel chair so he may swing to face the fish and unless it is below the gunwale, he should be strapped in because a hundred-pound pull might easily slide him overboard.

On the chair there should be a pivoting rod-seat, for the angler could not hold the rod in his hands and, with a belt-rest, his solar plexus will get a terrific mauling. He must have also a shoulder harness because neither hands nor arms could withstand the strain of hours of tussle with a big shark. Such a fight may last hours and if the angler does not feel equal to that, he had better stay "inside" and content himself with the smaller sharks.

TACKLE

For the smaller sharks, of about a hundred or even two hundred pounds, my usual tackle is a regular tuna rod (tip, five and a half feet, twelve ounces), 6/0 reel with nine hundred feet of No. 18 line.[1]

For the heavier fish, I use a swordfish rod, 9/0 reel, and twelve hundred feet of No. 24 line, or 12/0 reel with fifteen hundred feet of No. 30 or No. 36 line.

Apropos the size of lines, there is a great temptation to drift into using too heavy ones. A No. 39 line, with wet test of a hundred and seventeen pounds, might not seem any too strong for a five-hundred-pound shark, but the advantage of using it is more apparent than real.

A 9/0 reel will carry only eight hundred feet of it but it will

1. See Appendix II for explanation of rods, reels, lines, and tackle.

carry twelve hundred feet of No. 24 which has a wet test of seventy-two pounds. Properly handled, few fish are capable of putting such a pull on a line, especially if the line is long enough to give the boat a chance to turn, follow, and maneuver. I would rather take my chance with the additional four hundred feet of the lighter line than have my maneuvering restricted by the shorter though stronger one.

In my observation the greatest danger of losing the fish comes soon after the strike, before the boat is under way, or near the end of the fight, when he is being brought in for the iron.

To have the necessary strength at these critical moments and to enable one to carry at the same time the maximum length of line strong enough for the less strenuous intervals, I have adopted a scheme of "tapering" my line. The first three hundred feet from the hook is No. 24; the next six hundred feet is No. 21; and the last six hundred feet next to the reel is No. 18. It is seen, therefore, that I have fifteen hundred feet of line which, wet, will stand about fifty pounds when all is out, or about seventy pounds when only a hundred yards are out. I assume, of course, that the lines are spliced, for a knot is a weak point.[2,3]

With the lighter of these tackles, I use a 10/0 or a 12/0 O'Shaunessy or Van Vleck hook; with the heavier, a 14/0 Grinnell or a 13/0 Zane Grey.

At the hook there is ten inches of light phosphor-bronze chain to resist the grinding of powerful teeth, and between chain and line, fifteen or twenty feet of stainless steel cable (3/64) because the

2. For really large sharks, like those in the Bahamas, I use a 16-ounce-tip hickory rod, 12/0 reel, and 1200 feet of No. 36 line.

3. Tapered lines are now manufactured.

shark has an annoying trick of rolling to cut the line with fins or denticled hide. Both ends of the leader should be swivelled.

CHUM—BAIT

To attract sharks, bits of meat or fish may be tossed overboard to drift with the tide, or better, a chumming machine is used to grind alewifes or skates. Both of these are good, especially the skates, because they provide more blood with the oil. Sometimes, at a local slaughterhouse, it may be possible to get animal lungs and intestines, or blood, which make good "slick."

Almost any fish will do for bait, provided it is large enough, but I prefer skates and rays. The fish should be skinned and slashed and should be fresh.

METHODS

I have never had much luck trolling, except for Mackerel Sharks, unless I have happened to find sharks following a school of fish. In that case, the boat should "kick" along behind the school, which indicates the kind of bait to be used. Sharks caught in this way are likely to be of the fast surface-swimming species—let us hope for a White or a Mackerel Shark.

Still-fishing, you may anchor in the slick, or drift along with it, but if you anchor be sure to make fast your cable's end to a buoy carried on deck, which may be cast overboard, for there will be no time to up-anchor when a strike comes, nor will you be able to handle a big shark from an anchored boat.

If a fin appears, the bait may be "presented" as to a swordfish, but it is usually allowed to sink below the slick and to drift out fifty or a hundred yards. The heavy hook and leader are apt to carry the bait down to the bottom where crabs will be an infernal nuisance, so it is well to attach a wooden float or a rubber ball to the leader to hold the bait at the desired depth. The rubber ball performs other useful functions because as it rides on the rough surface it bobbles the bait, giving it a semblance of life and after the hook is "set" the buoyancy of the ball keeps a light tension on it, even if the shark gains slack line by running toward the boat.

THE FIGHT

The shark may hit the bait with a savage lunge, but except with the White or the Mackerel Shark, there is more likely to be a preliminary tugging. When this comes, slip the line a little, and, when he takes the hook, strike! And strike hard! He has a tough and leathery mouth.

Galvanized by the sting of the hook and infuriated by the check, away he goes in a wild straightaway. You can't stop him, so lie back in your harness, tighten down your drags, and put all safe pressure on the thumb-pad! Meantime, you are cussing the boatman to get under way and follow.

The boat takes a course parallel to that of the fish and about fifty yards away from it and you, by vigorous pumping, are trying to turn him and to recover some of the line he took out with his first rush.

After a mile or so, the shark and the boat, the one retarded by the pull of your line, and the other helped by it, may be almost abreast in the race and you may have turned him and started him

[53]

circling. It is your job now to keep him under constant tension, pulling his head toward the center of the circle of which your line is the radius while the boat follows on a smaller inside circle.

If you have in half of your line, to insure against another rush, there will be no immediate advantage in getting back more of it. On the contrary, it is better to keep the fish circling on a long radius to tire him out while you, lying back in your harness, save your strength for the fight to come.

There will be more rushes and more circling and, sooner or later, the shark will probably sound to the bottom and try to rub out the hook. Whether or not he could do this, he must not be allowed to lie there and rest. Your back may ache, your arms may be numb, your hands may burn, but you must "pump him up."

Sometimes a shark will suddenly cease pulling and will dash full speed toward the boat and past it, faster than you can reel in line. There is not much danger that he will throw the hook, but there is real danger that he may snap the line if he comes sharply to the end of the slack. You must throw off the free-spool lever and take on the strain gradually with the thumb-pad.

Toward the end, his rushes become shorter, his circlings smaller, and his soundings less mulish. He is tired and so are you! Finally, you get the double line up and then comes the steel cable. The boatman takes it and leads the shark to the boat side; the dart is poised and driven home. The lanyard whirls from the bucket. You drop back in the chair and light your pipe. What remains is the boatman's job!

For big sharks I prefer the harpoon, the swordfish dart, or the detachable head gaff, rather than the regular gaff. With them there is less danger from snapping jaws and threshing tail and the boatman might not be able to hold on to the gaff. Perhaps the gaff is more sportsmanlike and might be safely resorted to if the fight were prolonged to greater exhaustion of the fish and, incidentally, of the angler, but since the fight has already lasted several hours, it may be more humane to both man and fish to end it. Sometimes when a big powerful shark has been brought to the boat side on the dart-lanyard, I shoot him because he is a dangerous brute to take into the boat, and it is well-nigh impossible to judge when he is really dead. This may not be sportsmanlike, but it is prudent, and since the fight is over, nothing is lost by being sure the quarry is dead before he is put in the bag.

As I shall try to show, all sharks do not fight in the same way. In general, their tactics are like those of the tuna, for they rely mainly on power, though often they do show amazing bursts of speed. They rarely leap clear of the water, but they often breach the surface and go charging along it for long distances, dorsal and flukes showing in a smother of white foam. They usually pull away from the angler, but they may turn like a flash and dash toward the boat, compelling the man at the rod to think quick and act fast to save his line. Frequently they resort to that most difficult maneuver to meet successfully, stubborn soundings to the bottom for rest.

It must be admitted that for the angler all this involves lots of hard work, but he is out for sport and exercise and he gets both.

> There be some sports are painful, and their labour
> Delight in them sets off.—(*The Tempest.*)

THE GREAT WHITE SHARK

JAW OF A TIGER SHARK
This man weighs a hundred and seventy
pounds. Perhaps Linnaeus was right

CHAPTER VI

FIGHTS TYPICAL OF SPECIES

ON LIGHT TACKLE—A WHITE

C. RUSSELL BULL, whom I call Charlie, lives when not out in his boat, at Townsend, near the point of Cape Charles, Virginia. He is a fisherman and he would rather fish than eat, which is fortunate; for, having to eat, he makes his pleasure provide for his necessity. He had regarded nets, traps, and lines solely as means of capturing edible and marketable fish until I came along and proselytized him to the shark game and so diverted considerable of his time from more useful employment.

At first he knew as little as I about shark-fishing, which was indeed not much, but he was an apt follower of an enthusiastic leader and together, he at the wheel, and I in the chair, we learned until we became an efficiently working pair of "nuts" and a menace to the asterospondyli, which is a "high hat" name for sharks.

Charlie's boat, a twenty-foot navy "barge," is seaworthy, well-engined, reasonably fast and handy, and it immediately caught my eye as just the boat for the sport. Its after third is an open cockpit in which I put my chair, but a few feet from the wheel, to have the angler be within easy communication with the boatman who in turn is within arm's length of the engine controls.

Forward of the cockpit is a little cabin in which are two bunks, a hanging table and cooking paraphernalia. All is simple and neat. It is just a little fishing boat on which two people can live comfortably and, if necessary, two more can live uncomfortably.

[57]

Charlie is not only a good fisherman and a competent pilot, but he is also an excellent cook. When we sail we stock up with staples, take plenty of eggs, butter, milk, fruit, and vegetables. The waters teem with fish, oysters, and soft crabs. On our trips we have no schedule and we are not slaves to the clock. In fact, the clock is of minor concern, for it is the tide which regulates our lives. When it is right for fishing, we fish; when it is not right for fishing, we eat and sleep. Meals are prepared when more important matters do not demand attention. If weather be good, we stay outside; if it be bad we come in for shelter and stay there until it is better.

There is always infinite variety in the sea and in the waters opening upon it—"Age cannot wither nor custom stale her infinite variety"—and, for the man who loves them, there can be no monotony. With good company, good air, good food, good rest, and good sport, knocking around in a boat can be just about an ideal existence.

We are not always after sharks and for a change, or to rest tired muscles, we may turn toward drumfish, bluefish, weakfish, or any other variety that will take our bait. Hence the assortment of rods and tackle which clutters the little cabin.

We usually get plenty of these fish, but on one of our trips we utterly failed, and it was a shark which saved us from being "skunked."

At that season the big weakfish, or "tiders," averaging from five to nine pounds, good sport on light tackle, should have been running strong; but they were not. So we went outside and chummed for bluefish. There should have been schools of them off Smith's Island and the Isaacs; they were not there. Having so spent Monday and Tuesday, we trolled on Wednesday for drums, but they too failed us. Thursday, a nor'easter put all fishing out of the question until

Saturday, which turned out an ideal fishing day, with a light westerly breeze, but though we fished the channels and trolled along shore, our catch was nil. Sunday, my last day, with conditions perfect, found us two hours before sunset with but two fish—a pair of small weakfish.

We were then trolling for drum and had just come into Little Inlet, one of my favorite shark grounds, but it was six weeks too early for sharks and with a ten-ounce rod and No. 12 line, I was prepared for nothing heavier than drum. We were rolling along on the swell, hoping vainly for one of them to strike, when I spied a big fin. "Shark! Stop the boat!" I shouted, and Charlie throttled the engine. "You don't expect to get him on that outfit, do you?" But I was already rigging a wire leader and a big hook onto my little line. "We'll try!"

The tide drifted us back, the bait, one of my little weakfish, trailing along beneath the surface fifty yards astern. When it reached the place where I had seen the fin, there came along the line the characteristic tug of a shark. He had firm hold of the bait but had not taken the hook so I slipped him a few feet of line, and Bang! he took the hook and I struck. "Whee-w-wee-w!" went the reel, and I seemed to be fast to a speed boat. "Follow him!" and I put on all safe drag. The little 4/0 reel seemed to howl with pain and I expected the rod to snap at any moment, for I was giving them more than reasonable strain. The boat finally got up full speed and we were following the fish, but he had out all but ten yards of my line when he ceased to gain on us. Then, with the resistance I could give him, we began to gain, and in the next two miles I recovered half of my three hundred yards of line.

Steering off on a course parallel to that of the fish, in another mile we were abreast of him and I had him yielding and beginning to turn. He circled nicely a few times, but then, changing his mind, he went off into another rush of several miles before I could turn him again. When the circling recommenced, the tide was carrying us out rapidly, so we went spiralling toward Spain. "Are you prepared to serve breakfast on this ship?" I asked Charlie. "I see no probability of catching this minnow tonight." "Not unless you and the fish will give me a chance to cook it," he replied, and the shark, unconcerned about our breakfast, spiralled out further to sea.

Land was almost hull-down when he sounded, and lay still and Charlie, taking advantage of this armistice, slipped the harness onto me. Hardly was I thus geared when the shark woke up and went off into another long and furious rush which, however, was his swan song for after it he grew rapidly weaker. The harness was now giving me relief and I saw to it that the shark got none.

Throughout the struggle this shark had puzzled me for he was faster than any species I knew, except the Mackerel Shark, but the fleeting glimpses I had had of a blunt nose and a massive body showed that he was not a "Mackerel." When finally he was brought alongside, his fins and fluke stiff, and his body motionless, Charlie struck with the gaff but, stimulated by the pain, the shark wrenched the gaff from Charlie's hands and went down for another half hour of struggle. Twice more was this repeated but when he came up the fourth time Charlie, leaning over the gunwale, finished him with a butcher knife in the gills.

Now we had our first chance to recognize him. The dark spots on his pectorals, his olive ventrals, his ashy-brown back, white sides, caudal keels and triangular serrate teeth identified him as a small though beautiful specimen of the Great White Shark.

[60]

On the boat side he measured nine feet and two inches over all, and we estimated his weight as well over three hundred pounds. He had cost me a sprung rod and a damaged reel but he was worth it. His vitality had been amazing, but the fool fish had helped to catch himself, for it was his frantic rushes and hysterical circling which exhausted him. For long stretches he was on the surface with spray flying over his bow like that from an aquaplane. Nevertheless, it took two hours and forty-six minutes, from hook to gaff, to subdue him.

Perhaps I should be satisfied that he was a modest edition of this largest and most ferocious species of our North Atlantic, for the Great White Shark is said to attain a maximum length of more than forty feet. Such a shark could not be handled on a cable and one of half that size would make the fight almost hopeless on rod for it requires a skillful angler with the best of tackle to land a ten-footer.

The Great White Shark is essentially a rover of the broad ocean though small members of the species do sometimes follow schools of fish into bays and estuaries. He must be credited or discredited with being the true "Man-eater," for it is against him that naturalists have most conclusively sustained the murder charge. Linnaeus even indicted him as being the fish which swallowed Jonah, exonerating the whale as being incapable of taking a man down his gullet, though we now know that certain whales could do this.

Before Linnaeus, 1758, sixteen other scientists had declared that Jonah's whale was a shark and one of the earliest of these, Heinrich Herman Frey, in 1594, devoted nineteen pages of his book, *Icthyobiblia*, to this subject.[1]

1. A copy of this book, published in Leipsic, may be seen in the American Museum of Natural History, N.Y.

[61]

Even though one may not attach much importance to this question, it is interesting to learn how long and how vehemently this old controversy has continued though it is now probably of little importance to Jonah.

While but a minnow as compared with the prehistoric sharks, and much smaller even than the American Museum's megalodon, the largest White Shark of which I have heard in our times was enmeshed in the nets of the Ocean Leather Company at Cape Lookout, North Carolina, June, 1918.[2] This shark was credited with a length of twenty-two feet and a girth of eighteen feet and so would have weighed two and a half tons. Quite a fish for the nineteen hundreds!

It is a great temptation to go on writing about Whites and Mackerels, for there seems to have been an individuality in every one of them I have caught, but such a story would soon become simply "the same man caught another fish," and the reader, without the pitch of the boat, without the tang of the sea, without the whine of the reel, might be worse bored than I fear he now is, and besides I wish to tell about some other sharks.

DUSKY TACTICS

Duskies and Browns, which are somewhat like Duskies, do not fight in spirited rushes like Mackerels and Whites.

The Dusky (*Carcharibus obscurus*) is capable of considerable speed but he is more likely to base his stubborn defense upon his weight and power, and he thus deprives the angler of opportunity

2. Article by R. J. Coles in *Copeia*, American Society of Icthyologists and Herpotologists, May, 1919.

for making the fish wear himself out. If he simply sulks at the bottom and will not swim, the angler cannot make him circle. We might almost say that the Dusky does not work but makes the man work. If the angler does not force the fighting, the Dusky will simply offer passive resistance and apparently he could keep it up indefinitely. This calls for patience, skill, and strategy which lend interest to the fight with a Dusky though sometimes it recalls the old saying— "What's the use of kicking an elephant? you only wear out your shoe."

This shark is another suspected man-eater and certainly he is capable of being one for, averaging ten feet in length, he is stocky and powerful and his huge mouth is armed with dreadful teeth. Essentially a pelagic shark, he is nevertheless common to our inshore waters where he is not infrequently taken.

There is little trouble in identifying the Dusky because of his characteristic ashy-brown color, thick body, broad flattened snout, and extremely long falciform pectorals.

Among fisherfolk there is a tradition that he came to our shores during the Spanish-American War to avoid the gunfire in Cuban waters. Of course this is absurd, but he is often called the Santiago Shark.

One day, the Professor and I were chumming for bluefish fifteen miles off the New Jersey Coast and though we were not after sharks, our slick soon drew them. A sharp fin appeared, and then another and another until there were a dozen circling the boat at a respectful distance, close enough, however, to spoil our blue-fishing. I had aboard my tuna tackle, so baiting with a slashed bluefish, I began casting into the path of a large Hammerhead. He was, as usual, a very timid Hammerhead and he promptly drew off onto a

[63]

larger circle. Attaching the rubber ball to the leader, I let it float out. When the Hammerhead came around he was mildly interested but sank out of sight. A moment later there came a savage strike which sizzled off a hundred yards of line and then a hundred yards more with all drags down. "The Hammerhead!" I shouted—"Up anchor!" for I knew what a lively time that big Hammerhead would provide. Then the fish sounded and I knew it was not the Hammerhead for I recognized the sullen drag of a Dusky.

He now had out about three hundred yards of line and he would probably try to go no further, so settling into the harness, I prepared to spoil his rest. He yielded grudgingly and after a half hour of pumping I had him at the surface fifty yards away. Then down he went and his resistance redoubled. I dared not put strain enough on the tackle to lift him; plucking the line, banjo-string fashion, and tapping the rod failed to excite him into a move. He simply lay back with a dull straight tug, satisfied, apparently, to hold his own and let the other fellow get excited. I could picture him there at the bottom —twenty fathoms down—nose in the sand—tail toward the boat, "weaving" to resist my pumping. Presently he went off into a short leisurely surge, then stopped again, and I resumed pumping whenever the tackle would bear it.

"Dusky tactics," I groaned to the Professor, "and we are in for a long sweat of it!" In another half hour the shark was almost beneath the boat where he was endangering the line by "keel-hauling" it. Then I got him almost into dart range only to have him dive again. Over and over this performance was repeated and again and again split bamboo and cuttyhunk were severely tested before he got the iron. He was not a big shark, perhaps only six feet long, and he had not worked hard—but how he had made me work!

[64]

HAMMERHEAD
"A six foot man with a twelve
foot shark"

A BIG TIGER
Will provide shoes, bags, belts, ten
gallons of oil and shark fin soup

THE GREAT BLUE SHARK

These Dusky tactics do not provide excitement like those of Whites and Mackerels but they excel in requiring of the angler patience, judgment, and endurance. While I cannot really recommend the Dusky as a gamefish yet he does furnish the greatest test of self-control and, that failing, practice in language pardonable only to a fisherman *in extremis*. Also, a struggle with the Dusky should be good training for an oarsman or a stevedore. An angler friend of mine who asked why I wished to make a human derrick of myself must have seen a Dusky-fight.

On Heavy Tackle—A Great Blue

What was said of the Virginia Coast might almost as well apply to the entire Middle Atlantic Coast, and especially to the coast of New Jersey. There is a string of low islands and narrow sand strips standing off from the mainland as outposts against the onrush of the seas, and these separate from the ocean the almost continuous narrow sound which, in different places, we call by different names.

The water, too, has there the same gently rolling loveliness it has on the Chesapeake. There is a ripple, not a surge, to its movement and shadows from fleecy clouds, wafted by breezes laden with salt-marsh aroma, make myriad green tints on the surface. It is all so peacefully restful that even the gulls seem to dawdle in their flight. But through the inlets one bounds out onto the roaring blue ocean—What has all this to do with shark-fishing? Simply that the angler has his choice, as he had at Cape Charles. He may stay inside for little ones or he may go outside for big ones, but one of the uncertainties which go to make fishing interesting is that he may get the big one where he expected the little one, the little one where he expected the big one, or he may get neither.

I remember that, at the Virginia Capes, we had our angler lunching with John Smith, and the ships of the Jamestown settlers cut up his "slick." He will not meet John at Barnegat and the Indians killed most of those settlers long ago, but, musing, he may see explorers like Hendrik Hudson, Juan Caboto and others searching this coast for landing-places, or he may see founders like de la Warre sailing in to their new domains.

The altercation of the British and French fleets need not disturb him here though these waters are intimately associated with that fight he saw at the Virginia Capes. When de Grasse eluded Graves in the West Indies, Graves sailed along here hunting for him and then sailed back through these waters to meet de Grasse at the entrance of Chesapeake Bay and to be defeated there. Also, it was in these waters that Lord Howe played "puss-in-the-corner" with George Washington on land.

The fleet of transports which passed here en route to France from New York and Philadelphia is now replaced by a procession of peaceful coastwise merchant ships and frequently a Pacific liner bound for the Orient through the Panama Canal. Perhaps you could send shark fins on one of them to China.

We were out one day after tuna in these waters, trolling along over "The Ridge," an area of shallower soundings in the deep water off the Jersey Coast. My lure, flanked by the glittering splashing teasers, a hundred yards astern, skipped from crest to crest but it had failed to attract tuna, so at noon we had nothing to show but two large albacore.

A large Japanese steamer glided past, a quarter of a mile away, and across her white wake came cutting toward us a high triangular fin with rounded point. It ran so close alongside that its swis-s-s-h in the water was audible, while just below the surface, a long graceful form and a glint of blue suggested the species of its owner.

Dropping the tuna rod and seizing "Old Jim," my heavy tackle, I adjusted the ball close to the hook which John, the boatman, baited with half a bleeding albacore. When the shark came around in a circle he almost ran against the bait, floating on the surface twenty yards astern. He took it with a rush and headed straight out to sea. The whole thing was in plain sight. He had the hook. I did not need to strike, but I struck hard and, as we afterward learned, drove the big 14/0 Grinnell through the toughest part of the upper jaw where it held securely and where it interfered but little with the movements of the fish. The boat, too, was headed out to sea so we lost no time turning, and the engine "got the gun" immediately.

By heavy tackle, I mean that I was using heavy shark tackle, for any shark tackle might be called heavy, though it is not heavy for what it has to do.

Our three-ounce fly rods weigh a tenth as much as the trout we hope to catch on them and the lines will bear ten times the pull of a trout. If "Old Jim" were in that proportion it should weigh fifty pounds and the line should be a hawser.

I was especially glad that I was using what I have described as my "tapering line"; the first three hundred feet from the hook, No. 24; then six hundred feet of No. 21, and then six hundred feet of No. 18 to the reel; for this was an opportunity to test it. Notwithstanding our prompt start, and in spite of the resistance of the drags, the shark had out all of the No. 24 before we got up headway and when we had full speed he was out on the No. 18, a quarter of a mile away. Veering so as to take the fish over the starboard bow, retarding him with a fifty-pound pull, which also helped the boat, now forced ahead with open throttle, we held our own for five miles. Then we edged away to get a sidewise pull which finally turned the shark so that he began to circle as an amenable shark should do.

For an hour he raced around his course, covering more than a mile at each lap, in a surge of white foam, while we, at easy speed, followed on an inside circle. I had only to hold my end of the line against the resistance of the water to keep him circling. After about fifteen miles of this I tried to bring him closer but as he was not ready to come, I left him out on the big circle for more exercise. When he showed signs of weakening by slowing his pace, I pumped him in to the No. 21 line and then nagged him to greater effort and later brought him to the No. 24 where I "treated him rough." All through the fight this fish acted like a well-trained race horse, simply charging along his course with never an attempt to fly the track and I am glad that he never tried to sound for I did not know how deep the water was out there. When at last the iron was thrown, it struck in the vital gills and he died without undue commotion.

The aggressive and fearless way in which this Blue approached the boat and took the bait was characteristic of his species. The Blue Shark seems to have little dread of man and is the shark that gives most trouble to the whalers in their "cutting in" of the blubber for he is so bold in his dashes at the carcass that often he must be fought back with blubber-spades. Also, it may be mentioned as apropos of what has been said of ferocity and cannibalism among sharks, that those wounded by the spades are invariably killed and devoured by their companions.

The Great Blue, though a warm-water species, frequently cruises along our coast but he also ranges the wide ocean. It is usually this species that follows ships at sea; it is about the Great Blue that most of the sea shark-stories are told, and he is the source of sailor superstitions. Familiar among these is the belief that sharks follow a ship on which there is a dead sailor—perhaps they do, for in all probability they would be following it anyway.

HAMMERHEAD TRICKS

It may be remembered that it was a Hammerhead on the Chesapeake which literally towed me into this shark-fishing game, but it is not that alone which is responsible for the thrill I always experience when fast to a Hammerhead. He is a wary suspicious fellow who is hard to outsmart and he has gamefish qualities equalled by few other sharks.

This strange fish may have come down from some member of the Requiem group of sharks (Sand Sharks, Blues, etc.) whose slender body and pointed snout he exhibits in exaggerated form, while his flattened head extends to both sides in thin vanes that give him exactly the outline of a blacksmith's hammer on its helve.

Nature, always with a purpose in what she does, has given the fish this freakish head to be used for making his dives and loops, as ailerons are used on an airplane, and so erratic are his gyrations that once—I hesitate to tell it—a Hammerhead tied a knot in my line. I hasten to explain, however, it was a simple knot, not a bowline.

In contrast to other sharks, most of which have rather small, staring, amber eyes, the eyes of the Hammerhead, located in the outer edges of the vanes, are large, dark, and bovine, but please do not imagine that I am trying to make out a case of gentleness for him for he is, as his bladelike teeth indicate, as savage as other sharks, and as mean a devil as any of them.

[69]

Hammerheads are said to reach a length of eighteen feet though ten feet would be perhaps an average length for a large one. Because of their slender build, they are, however, lighter than other sharks of the same length.

They are top-swimmers, live-fish-feeders, and as their lithe shape suggests, they are exceedingly fast.

The finest struggle I ever had with a Hammerhead was one day on a glassy sea ten miles off the New Jersey Coast when we spied a high sharp dorsal, "gaff topsail" sailors call it, cutting the surface half a mile astern and following straight in our wake. Slowing down our engine, I let out three hundred yards of line baited with a fair-sized bluefish. As the bait skittered along on the surface the Hammerhead overtook it, circled it and came on. There was really no disappointment in this because it was exactly what a man, familiar with this wary fish, would expect. We opened throttle, dragged the bait past the fin, and this time the shark dashed at it, splashed around it, showed great interest, but was still too timid to strike so we slowed down and then—Bang! He had it! On he came straight for us while I wound frantically. Fifty yards astern he seemed to associate us with his toothache; increasing speed, he swung wide around us, and I wound hard to take up the great bellying sag in the line. With the fish a hundred yards to port, the line came straight. I threw off the free spindle lever, thumbed the pad, screwed down drags, struck hard to set the hook and then—what a performance!

Straight toward us dashed the fish, whirling and pitching on the surface, barely clearing our bow. Then away he went—two hundred yards to the other side while the boatman, leaving his wheel, clambered atop the deckhouse to clear the line. Like a flash he turned and was back again, just clearing the stern while John, the

[70]

boatman, fended the looped line from the propeller with a boat hook and I struggled in vain to take in slack. Again and again this was repeated and then the Hammerhead changed his tactics to short dashes back and forth on the surface, and dives and loops beneath it; once, in spite of our backing and turning, he went under the boat.

He had not been allowed to put much strain on the line but he was entirely too lively to fight at close range; so as soon as we could, we worked away on a long line where we could keep him under tension with the boat.

John had had a lot of practice with his engine and rudder, my wrist ached from winding and my thumb burned from the hot pad when we finally got the fish to circling. After an hour of that, the big gaff hook drove into his gills and the fight was over. It had been like a tarpon-fight except that this demon was bigger and stronger than any tarpon, and he looped in the water instead of going into the air. Hammerheads are wary, fast, and game but I have never seen any fish put up a finer fight than this one did, from hook to gaff. I forgot to measure and weigh this shark so I can give only my estimate—9 feet, 250 pounds.

TACTICS OF DIFFERENT SPECIES

I wish I could include here accounts of the fighting of the Mako (*Isuropsis mako*) of the South Seas which is admittedly the sport-fish par excellence of all selachians but I have caught but two or three of them and am not qualified to discuss them. I believe, however, that even that experience justifies me in concurring with Zane Grey that the Mako is "a premier sporting fish, as game as beautiful, as ferocious as enduring."

[71]

Dr. Grey published in *Natural History*, June, 1934, an account of his fishing for Mako in New Zealand, where he tells of the characteristic fight of this great fish which combines the tactics of tarpon, swordfish, and shark.

From the accounts of my struggles with sharks on the line, I have omitted those with the less sporty varieties and have told of but one fight typical of each species. Characteristic as I believe these tactics to be, they are not to be taken as illustrating fixed methods by which the various sharks fight, for, while each species seems to have a characteristic method, it is not averse to using the tricks of others.

The White and the Mackerel, of which I told, used speed and power out on a long line, sometimes at the surface, sometimes down, and they resorted to sounding. The Blue, a little slower than these, used about the same tactics though he did not sound. The Dusky did little rushing, stayed closer to the boat, and, from the beginning, sulked mulishly at the bottom. The Hammerhead, on the other hand, made neither long rushes nor soundings but dashed frantically back and forth on the surface or dived and looped beneath it. Yet, I have seen Duskies run, Mackerels sulk, and Hammerheads sound. All of them are vital, powerful, and enduring, so if the fight were to be a test of mere brute strength, the man would be licked before he got well started.

Unfortunately for the fish, however, the man has more brains, and even an angler is expected to show more intelligence than a shark who, furthermore, is at a disadvantage. Reversing conditions, suppose the man in the cockpit to have a 14/0 Grinnell in his mouth while the shark, comfortably harnessed, tugs at the line to pull him overboard. How many hours would the contest last? Before the shark could call to the ray—"Give him the spear!" Then, hanging the man's jaws on a coral branch, they could discuss the fighting qualities of the human species—"Which is the gamest, Jew or Gentile, Ethiopian or Indian?"

CHAPTER VII

TO THE LAIR OF THE TIGER SHARK

STUDY had verified for me the tradition that the waters of the West Indies are the habitat of sharks in great numbers, of many species of unusual size and ferocity, and I was anxious to have a try at them with rod and reel. Through Mr. H. S. Mazet, co-author with Captain Young of a recent book, *Shark! Shark!*, I met Mr. Gillette, President of The National Fisheries Corporation, a commercial company engaged in shark-fishing, and I was soon in correspondence with the resident manager of the company at Nassau, Mr. E. M. Schuetz. Him I found to be not only thoroughly informed as to sharks but also to be a sportsman, ready to help us with the preparation of the little expedition which I was planning.

According to Schuetz, the Bahamas were "lousy" with sharks —Sand Sharks, Nurse Sharks, Black Tips, Duskies, Blues, Browns, Hammerheads, and Tigers. His information was not based on casual rumor but came from his records of the thousands of sharks caught by him for his company. I think, however, that Schuetz was a little nonplussed at the idea of fishing for sharks as sport-fish with rod and reel. Nevertheless, he got my idea and he thought that the Bahaman Tigers would give me all the fight I was looking for. "Tiger Shark!" The very name sends cold chills through the marrow of a Carib and pictures to the shark-hunter the great brute which it so well describes.

Schuetz reported them large, savage, and abundant. A letter from him told of the return of one of his parties with fifty-one sharks; thirty-one of them Tigers, two fourteen-footers and one sixteen-footer. That letter settled me—I was going! A sixteen-foot Tiger would weigh upwards of a ton and could not be held on a rod, but what fun trying to do it! The ten-footers, weighing six or seven hundred pounds, could be handled.

News went to Schuetz that we were coming and he began looking up a boat for us.

My son, Hugh, is as keen a sportsman, or should I say "fishing crank," as is his father. My son, John, a Princeton undergraduate, is deeply interested in biology, and since Professor Dahlgren, of the Biology Department, Princeton University, could not go with us, John had to be our biologist, but Dahlgren wrote a letter bespeaking for us interest and help. J. Victor Coty, the lecturer on fishing and an expert movie cameraman, joined us to take movies of the sport, undeterred by his experience in roughing it with Dahlgren and me before.

People who are unfamiliar with the tropics invariably have exaggerated ideas of the heat, so we were the recipients of the usual criticism for having selected summer as the time to visit Nassau. Had we wished to do so, we could not have avoided this, because we were after sharks and midsummer is the best season for them, and later in the year hurricanes make being out in a small boat impracticable. As a matter of fact, however, the heat in Nassau is no worse than that of midsummer in New York and the thick-walled high-ceilinged houses with broad shaded verandas surrounded by palm trees make it endurable. Sitting in the shade of palms, fanned by ocean breezes, and sipping a Planter's Punch, one can really pity people at home.

June 16, our party, equipped with eight rods, miles of line,

SHIPS GREETED BY BOATLOADS OF DIVERS
None are ever hurt by sharks

ANDROS ISLAND
Where pirates rendezvoused and
where modern swashbucklers still dominate
the depths

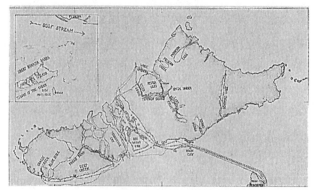

Courtesy of New York Zoological Society

MAP OF ANDROS ISLAND

and dozens of hooks and leaders; harpoons, harness, and tackle-boxes; silk nets and bottles of formaldehyde for the biologist; endless paraphernalia for the photographer, and, incidentally, some clothing; embarked on the "Munargo" at New York. Bound on such an expedition, we were naturally more or less curiosities to other passengers but their interest in our doings was rather surprising. On the passage we were kept busy answering questions like: "How big are sharks? Do they really attack boats? Do they eat men?" One young man was nervous about them on bathing beaches and wanted to know if there was much danger from sharks in the water at Coney Island. "Not as much," I replied, "as there is from rusty old tin cans, but *bottles* are probably the greatest danger there." "Suppose a shark jumps into your boat?" asked one girl, in perfect seriousness. "Then," said I, "I should write an article, for that would be news."

NASSAU

Two and a half days out from New York we slid into the amethyst Harbor of Nassau to be greeted by a score of dinghies each laden with chattering, shouting, native boys who howled that coins be tossed for them to dive after. Now, these waters are infested with sharks but the boys are never hurt by them. They are really in no danger from sharks because the shark is, in fact, a timid creature which keeps away from such commotion as is going on. If the sharks were chummed up and excited by the scent of food or blood, these boys would not last long, but as it is they have little to fear. I would readily insure them for a very small premium but I would not go in there with them for a considerable sum. There you have one of those anomalies which apparently attach to most shark lore. The government seems to recognize the element of safety in the noise and crowd of the harbor, for it forbids these boys to ply their trade outside.

While we hung over the rail watching these aquatics in which the prizes go immediately to the most efficient, Mr. Schuetz bustled aboard to meet us—clean shaven, in a crisp linen suit and wearing a straw hat—the typical business-man of the tropics. He was so bubbling over with interest and so generous with his help that, after thanking him for what he had already done, I could not resist asking why he was so good. "Because," said he, "I am a sportsman and I like to help other sportsmen," and certainly, while we were in the Bahamas, he lived up to that ideal.

Tackle and equipment unloaded, Hugh and I went across the dock to look over the boats that Schuetz was holding tentatively for us and selected the "Malolo B.", a thirty-nine foot modified "sea-skiff." She was sound, clean, and well engined; there were bunks for four, galley, toilet, and facilities for food and ice storage. Aft there was a roomy cockpit and two swivel chairs. What appealed to me immediately was that the helmsman's wheel, in easy reach of all controls, was forward of the chairs but in plain view of them. There were some details about the boat which might have been better, for example: there was no hoisting crane for taking aboard big fish, but all in all, she was surprisingly well suited to our purposes, and it must be remembered that our demands were unusual.

No one at Nassau had ever seen sharks angled for with rod and reel and the ideas of John and Coty had never risen above their horizon. Altogether, we were undoubtedly pioneers but the natives probably regarded us as a bunch of "nuts." At first the boatmen, though politely humoring us, clearly could not understand, and Schuetz alone seemed to get our idea.

[78]

It was unfortunate that the light top deck came so far aft over the cockpit that the cameraman, perched on it, had not a very satisfactory place for "shooting" at the rodman. This, however, may have been fortunate for the cameraman because the rodman could not shoot him. Let me say here, to the credit of Victory Coty, that there never was but one time when we wished to shoot him. That was when Hugh, after an hour or more of fight, was barely managing to hold a nine-hundred-pound Tiger at the surface, fifty feet away. The shark persisted in working around on the port side while Coty was all prepared on the starboard. "Lead him around to this side where the light is better!" called Coty, sticking his head over the awning edge. I omit replies from the chair.

But to return to our preparations! The captain, Lattie Kemp, and his helper, Burton Bowe, were left to make the boat ready and to store the supplies, which Mrs. Wise, acting as chandler, had ordered from "Sands," and then Hugh and I went to join her and John at the hotel.

When one steps ashore in Nassau, he is at once impressed with the ease and comfort which the population, mainly black, enjoys.

Along the main street, paralleling the shore, the small stone and wooden houses are closely jammed together, but on the streets leading from it there is more room and there are some small pretty houses.

Apparently there was little architectural thought expended in building Nassau, landscaping was likewise lightly considered and city authorities just let the town "grow up like Topsy." All this may be, in part, due to disinclination to build and beautify in defiance of the devastating storms and hurricanes for which the Bahamas are famous.

TIGERS OF THE SEA

The most conspicuous flight of the architectural imagination seems to have been indulged in the modest but handsome palace of the Governor and there is literally a flight—a hundred or more steps lead up to it. St. Peter, in this respect, has nothing on the Governor of the Bahamas.

As in other British colonies, the streets are clean, but how narrow they are! cars pass cautiously, and at corners they must stop and honk before turning. One never knows what he may meet around a corner—a bicycle, a donkey-cart, or a wheeled sponge-crate, and all vehicles keep to the left of the road, thus adding to the American's confusion. Horse-drawn surreys are still a popular means of transportation in Nassau, so when Hugh and I had finished our arrangements at the boat we chartered a surrey to take us to the hotel, but when the poor old horse could not pull us up the hill, the driver descended from the box and pulled with him.

With its abundance of tropical foliage Nassau is quaintly and exotically attractive. Sponge marketing, the most important industry of Nassau, is interesting, though drab in color; but another, grass-weaving, fills the street markets with pretty baskets and bright-colored hats, which are urged by the native women vendors on the visitor. Our party purchased some of these, but was saved from buying hundreds of them only by the greatest self-denial. Hugh's photographs show him fishing under the shade of a gaudy headgear which was evidently intended for a black Nassau belle.

We were there, of course, out of season, so most of the big hotels were closed, and we made our headquarters at the old Royal Victoria which, with flagstone terraces, wide balconies, in general rambling design, and total disregard of space, is distinctly tropical.

There were few other people in the hotel and no entertainment was attempted for the guests. But while we were having dinner on the terrace and talking over our plans with Mr. Schuetz, a black troubadour with a one-stringed guitar leaned against a palm tree and repeated a verse about his mother who "don't want no peas, no rice, no cocoa-nut oil" until we paid him to quit. A week later, when we were there again we had to get rid of him in the same way.

During the day Schuetz had given us all possible instructions and mainly on his advice we decided to start our shark hunt at Andros Island. Hugh and I went aboard after dinner at the hotel, ready to sail at daylight, the boat, equipment, and tackle all checked and the charts studied.

OFF TO ANDROS ISLAND

Nothing could have been more propitious than our start at dawn on that beautiful morning. Out of the placid harbor, our engine purring rhythmically, we glided onto a gently rolling sea. Green palms fringing the coral shore nodded farewell in the gentle breeze, and houses pink in the rising sunlight blinked good luck.

Those broad inland waterways between the Bahaman Islands surpass all description, for, exquisite as are the pastel tints along the shores, still more beautiful are the shades of blue and green separated from them by the line of feathery, foaming white breakers, and, over all, great drifting masses of cumuli, glistening white, silver, rose, and gold beneath an azure sky. The breath of early sunlit morning is in the breeze which soothes the temples, the tang of the sea is in the spray which feels good on face and tastes good on lips. The very bound of the boat seems to lift one's soul above all that is on drab land.

Bearing away from New Providence Island, land sinks from view beneath a rolling sea which now in full daylight takes on in one direction the deep blue of the Mediterranean and, in another, the brilliant green of the Chesapeake.

Poets and artists would stop the engine to lie here and drink in all this loveliness, but we are only fishermen so we open the throttle and drive on toward the sport of which we have been dreaming. Southwest we head, fifty miles to Andros Island, the former rendezvous of famous pirates and still the habitat of giant sharks, swashbucklers of the sea as bloodthirsty and as relentless to other fishes as were Morgan and Blackbeard to men.

Now running along close enough to the Andros shore to hear the surf booming on its coral edge, one falls to musing that on these same swells rode the ships of those old buccaneers, that behind this island they awaited their merchant-ship prey, that on these shores were held the drunken orgies when loot was divided and that into these crystal waters plunged the victims who walked the plank—to be devoured perhaps by the ancestors of the very sharks we are hunting.

Privateers, Pirates, Buccaneers, and Bootleggers

Pirate traditions cannot be disassociated from Bahaman folklore, because for a long period the Jolly Roger, if not the legitimate ruling flag of the islands, was nevertheless the actually dominant flag. One can of course find nothing admirable about these pirates but there is a glamour in their exploits which does hold the imagination and which invests them in the eyes of the natives with a kind of heroism. In spite of civilization, a red-blooded man's heart may kindle to the spirit of daring self-reliance even in a pirate whom he detests, and perhaps Morgan has no more admirers in the Bahamas than Jesse James has in our own country.

But piracy in the Bahamas was more than a casual or exceptional enterprise, for it was the profession of no inconsiderable part of the population in league with the sea-rovers who rendezvoused there. Even before the sway of the pirates a prevalent occupation of the islands was scarcely more "regular," except that it was authorized, for the Bahamas were a base of operations for the privateers of Henry VIII who waylaid Spanish galleons and hijacked from them the stolen gold they were taking home from South America. Far be it, however, for the scion of Devonshire ancestors to call those worthies *pirates*. They were commissioned by the King—they were *privateers*. One wonders, nevertheless, whether this training did not predispose those crews for service, later, under Jolly Roger. When Spain had lost her sea power, and there were no more Spanish galleons to rob, and when Great Britain had made piracy an undesirable occupation, there must have been a slump of business in the Bahamas until the American Revolution offered opportunity for gun-running and ammunition-smuggling. Later, our Civil War gave another boost to trade in the Bahamas, for the islands then became an important source of supply for the Confederate Army and their waters became the rendezvous of innumerable blockade runners.

Then there was a long slump until the Eighteenth Amendment brought trade back to Nassau and Bimini, and wealth to their inhabitants. Now, that repeal has ruined this trade, many fast rum-runners have had to be converted into prosaic fishing boats. What a checkered career these placid islands have had!

On the run across, assisted by Burt, I was laying out and assembling tackles for bait-fishing and shark-fishing and at the same time instructing him. His eyes fairly danced with delight at the sturdy rods, big reels and handsome gear with which he was hitherto unfamiliar but which he was soon to understand, for that boy was a natural born angler. He knew the waters, had an uncanny way of finding fish, and before the week had passed he could bait a hook, throw a dart or noose a tail as well as any boatman I ever had.

Fondly stroking a big rod as he hung it up in its cradle, he said: "Kunnel, we are going to have good luck." "Luck!" I replied, "Burt, there is no such thing as luck." "Yessuh?" "If we go to the proper place, at the correct time, with the appropriate tackle and the right bait and if we know how to fish, we will get fish." "Yessuh!" "If from ignorance or through neglect, we fail to do what we should do, or if we laze through our fishing, we will not get fish." "Nosuh." "Then we will say that we had bad luck. That word 'luck' is simply a symbol by which we try to express something we do not understand or won't admit." "Yessuh." I could almost hear Burt's brain gears buzz as he tried to master this idea, which I confess I myself did not quite understand and which I had enunciated mainly to forestall any fisherman alibi which might be forthcoming later. Burt disappeared below, but on returning in a few minutes with some more paraphernalia, he squared himself in front of me and said: "Kunnel, we are going to have good lu—, I mean we are going to get fish, because we have done everything you say we ought to do and the day and the weather are just perfect." By which statement Burt proved himself to be an optimist and a diplomat.

Courtesy of Dr. E. W. Gudger

BAIT
The Barracuda or the Boy.

CHAPTER VIII

AMONG THE TIGERS

AT noon we slowed down off High Cay to troll for bait, but this is not the drudgery one might think it to be, for the bait was barracuda and that big game fish is itself well worth coming for. Not to miss any of the sport, we used our light tarpon rods and made the most of the fights.

In grace, speed, power and ferocity the barracuda yields to few fish. On tackle he has been taken weighing more than a hundred pounds, though usually his weight is scarcely one-fifth of that. Ours averaged about ten or fifteen pounds, but they struck with a terrific lunge and fought like demons until they were gaffed.

Barracudas are as savage as sharks and as relentless in the toll they take of other fish. About the only thing in the sea which they will not attack is the shark, for about the only thing they cannot tear with their terrible spiked teeth is the denticled hide of a shark. The barracuda is really more to be feared than the shark because he can and does frequent the shallow waters of bathing beaches where deaths and injuries inflicted by barracudas far exceed those inflicted by sharks who are blamed for many of them.

There is a mistaken idea that shark bait may be any old meat, fish, or flesh, but the shark prefers bait in which there are traces of at least recent life. Barracuda is particularly good bait, because for a long time it oozes blood and gives off a strong oily scent. It is best to catch them and to use them fresh, and it would have been difficult to buy them, because, about Andros, fishermen were scarce.

Though we fished but one line for sharks, we always worked from both chairs for bait, so Hugh and I went to it with medium tackle, baited with small fish, locally called "Goggle Eyes."

Hardly were our lines out when a big barracuda struck and sizzled off two hundred yards of Hugh's line in a glorious run. Then my reel shrieked and a big barracuda took out two-thirds of my line before I checked him. In about ten minutes I had him coming and within a hundred yards of the boat, when a shout went up— "There's a shark after him!" The barracuda leaped and came down into the white surge which followed him, an added strain came on my twelve-strand line and my rod bent into a semi-circle. Then the line slacked and I wound in a barracuda's head, the shark having kept the rest of the fish as his share. It must have been a Mackerel Shark because we were trolling at about five miles an hour and other sharks rarely strike at such trolling speed.

I changed to a ten-ounce-tip tuna rod and a fifteen-strand line, and let out in hopes of having the shark strike again. In the meantime, Hugh had hung onto a twenty-pound grouper and was handling him handsomely; and now something that felt like a whale took hold of my line and started off with a slow relentless tug which would have demolished the tackle I had just discarded. The boat was stopped, and while Hugh went on catching barracudas I fought my strike for half an hour. Then my fish sounded and could not be budged. Peering through the water glass over the boat side, Burt spotted him as a huge jewfish, weighing probably four hundred pounds; but he was down in a coral crevice, so we had to cut him loose.

[86]

Poison Fish

One of the barracudas we had caught was such a beautiful specimen that Burt, looking at him, remarked—"He looks good enough to eat." "Certainly," I replied, "we will eat him tonight." "No!" shouted he and the captain in horrified chorus. "He's poisonous!" I had always thought that fish-poisoning was entirely due to the ptomaines of partial decomposition and knowing that this fish was fresh, I attributed their protest to native superstition, but I humored them and we did not eat the barracuda. Later inquiry proved, however, that this belief was general in the Bahamas, so on my return to New York, I reported it to Dr. Gudger of the American Museum and then I learned how ignorant I had been, for in the West Indies there is a well-known disease, *Ciguatera*, caused by the eating of certain fish, among them barracudas, whose flesh, particularly in the breeding season, may be impregnated with toxic secretions."[1,2]

In Japan more advance has been made in the study of this disease than with us, but Dr. Walker of the U. S. Navy, Dr. Georgagan of Bermuda, Mr. Mowbray of the Bermuda Aquarium and others have made much headway and have adduced sufficient proof for us laymen that there is this toxic poisoning, distinct from ptomaine poisoning. So I learned that Burt's fear was well founded.

While we are on this subject, it may be worth noting that the severity of wounds and cuts from fish spines and fins is not necessarily due to infection, as is generally supposed. Certain catfish, for example, secrete from glands at the bases of the pectoral fins, a

1. Gudger, Dr. E. W., *Poisonous Fishes and Fish Poisons*, Am. Mus. Natl. History.

2. *Am. Journal of Tropical Medicine*, Vol. 1, No. 1.

specific poison, and the stingray is provided with glands that poison the wounds made by his spike so that the effect is comparable to the bite of a venomous snake though usually less dangerous.

What satisfaction it must now be to John Smith, safe in his sailor's rest, to know that the world can no longer attribute his long illness after the stingray wound to ignorance and lack of cleanliness! Poor old John! He has been held up for several centuries as a horrible example of what might happen to little boys who do not take care of their "fishin' cuts."

First Shark Blood

With enough bait, and having had great sport getting it, we dropped over to the shark grounds in the channel, slowing down to lay a slick as we drew near.

I was first in the chair, and Burt put half a barracuda on my hook. Before we came to a stop and while Burt still stood holding my baited hook in his hand, a big fin came up in the streak twenty-five yards astern. "Throw it!" I yelled, and "Plop!" it hit the water a few yards in front of the fin. A swirl—a rush—he had it! I struck, and out went the line with the high-pitched whine of the reel while Hugh strapped me to the chair. We had a great fight, that shark and I, or rather I did, before his ugly Tiger mouth showed at the surface ten feet away about an hour later. It was Burt's first throw but he drove the dart deep just above the pectoral fin and as the lanyard whirled from the bucket, he gradually snubbed it around a cleat. Then the shark was hauled in for the killing lance and a noose was slipped around his tail and he was swung up to a stanchion and split open to freshen up the slick with his blood and oil.

[88]

"First Blood!" and there was plenty of it on the boat and on the water.

When we came back to the slick I surrendered the chair to Hugh who immediately became engaged in battle with another three-hundred-pound Tiger. He had a more difficult job than I had had, because we had anchored to hold against the tide and the anchor was down when he got his strike. We could not get it aboard, and dangling aweigh three fathoms below the bow, it seriously interfered with our maneuvering. Nevertheless Hugh brought his fish to iron in good style.

We both had tired backs when we quit to make the anchorage before dark behind the reef at Mangrove Cay. We had come after Tigers and here they were. There was one slender fish of about fifty pounds which still showed the leopard spots characteristic of young Tiger Sharks. The second, weighing about three hundred pounds, had distinct tiger stripes on his sturdy body, and the third, about the same size but evidently older, was of uniform brownish-grey, showing indistinct stripes only near his tail. Both of the larger ones were vicious devils and when their blunt noses came up their big jaws with cruel sickle-shaped serrate teeth were snapping like bear traps and we understood the dread they inspired in the natives.

When we anchored at Mangrove Cay I stretched out luxuriously in a deck chair and volunteered to keep ship while the rest of the party went ashore to call on the British Commissioner. Their dinghy had hardly reached the beach when I began to regret my decision, for our captain had anchored us behind a little wooded point where the mosquitoes were undisturbed in their activities by any breeze. You could not have paid a penny each for those mosquitoes with a fund equal to our national debt and I was convinced that every one of them took a dig at me. The most irritating thing about it all, except the stinging burning bites, was that a hundred yards away the water rippled with a good breeze and there were no mosquitoes. There is no need of repeating my remarks to the captain when he returned.

The presence of a party like ours in harbor at Mangrove Cay is quite an event so I received many callers who paddled out to satisfy their curiosity, and whom I energetically pumped to satisfy mine. When the shore party returned they brought some turtle meat, *langouste*, fresh fruit, and a gunny sack full of green cocoanuts whose milk, that most refreshing of tropical drinks, served us well in the days to come.

MANGROVE CAY

This is a native town of about twelve hundred inhabitants which stretches in a single row of palm-thatched houses for nine miles along the shore. Mr. Forsythe, the British Commissioner, is, I believe, the only white man there but he seems to like it for he has been there twenty years. Mangrove Cay is his kingdom where he is ruler, counselor, friend, and advisor to all, in sickness and in health—one of those Englishmen who extend British influence more, perhaps, than it is carried by conquest.

The natives are a mixture of Carib and Negro, varying in type between the two. Some of them appear to be pure Carib, with thin nose, high cheek bones, straight hair and bronze skin while others are distinctly West Indian negroes. All of them impress the visitor by their kindliness and good humor even more than they surprise him by their ignorance. Their friendliness to us was demonstrated by their insistence upon a ball in our honor. Of course we were expected to pay the musicians—one of their popular songs carries the refrain, "Fine gal, take care of the rich man sailor."

Andros Island is some hundred miles long and forty wide, but very low. From natives we learned of fresh-water lakes in the interior in which were to be found sharks, barracudas and other pelagic fishes which, of course, may have been swept overland into them by great hurricane waves. The sharks are reputed to be of great size and ferocity, so fierce, the natives said, that the government had warned the people to avoid those waters, but I am inclined to believe that such sharks, if or when there, are but trapped and temporary sojourners rather than permanent residents and that, sooner or later, they will succumb to these unusual conditions.[3]

The physiological processes of sharks are apparently not so well adapted to life in fresh water as are those of some other fishes, various teleosts for example. Certain small rays are known to live permanently in some fresh-water rivers of South America, sharks do ascend the Ganges far above salt water and sharks are found in the land-locked fresh water of Lake Nicaragua. There is considerable doubt, however, among scientists as to whether these Nicaragua sharks are a misidentified form of wanderer from the sea or whether they are a fresh-water species.

Mr. C. M. Breder, Jr., Assistant Director, New York Aquarium, spent some time on Andros Island and he informs me that, though he heard these same stories of sharks in the fresh-water lakes, he saw nothing of them nor of barracudas, although he did find many other pelagic fish in them.

It would have been most interesting to investigate these rumors

3. Report of C. M. Breder, Jr., "Ecology of Fresh Water Lakes, Andros Island," N. Y. Zoological Society, Vol. XVIII, No. 3.

by a visit to the interior of the island and also to see there the great flamingo flocks, but really, that was not the immediate purpose of our trip, so we returned to the "Malolo" and turned in on deck to rest for shark-fights on the morrow.

Sleep does not dally in coming to the healthily tired man in balmy sea air under starry sky. It seemed but a moment when the crowing of a rooster somewhere ashore was answered by a chorus of challenges from other cocks in the village while the grey horizon changed to pink. A plunge overboard, overalls pulled on, and our toilets were complete. Anchor up and we were away with the aroma of boiling coffee and sizzling bacon rising from the little galley to start the joy of the day.

AT SOUTH BIGHT

On this day, June 21, we passed out through the reef-opening and started trolling for bait with our usual good luck and fine sport. Let me repeat that a big barracuda on a ten-ounce rod is not to be sneered at as a game fish even when he is to be used for shark bait, and also that day we got some fine yellowtails which we hated to see ground up for chum. One of them, fighting on the line, leaped from the water, and leaping after him, a barracuda cut him in two. Coty had his camera focussed on the yellowtail and got a picture of this which shows in the movie but unfortunately the negative does not enlarge into a good still picture.

We got to shark-fishing at about eleven o'clock opposite the entrance to South Bight. Hugh, in the chair, had slipped his bait only twenty yards from the boat when it was struck hard, and Hugh, squeezing down drags, slowed down the run till the reel sang only a low baritone. Meantime, Burt, out in the dory with the water glass, got a view of the fish. "It's a medium-sized Mackerel Shark," he called, "and there's a whole string of others following. One of 'em is longer than the dory!"

The water was beautifully clear, and without the glass we could see several sharks close to the boat—the chum was certainly working on them!

By this time, Hugh's Mackerel was breaching and churning at such a rate that our attention centered on him. For three-quarters of an hour Hugh pumped and slipped line while Lattie at the wheel had the boat doing a waltz. Finally, the sharp nose and long dorsal came up close enough to the boat for Burt to throw the dart and a few minutes later the shark, tied to the stanchion, was oiling the waters he had so troubled.

Now it was my turn in the chair. There were so many sharks around us that it was like flock shooting, and one nailed my bait almost immediately. But I struck too soon—drove the hook before it was well in the mouth, and in a few minutes, brought up a piece of lip.

Then, with a fresh bait, I got a determined sullen tug. I gave this fellow time then struck hard. As the hook drove in there came a resistless rush which tested the No. 30 to the limit and bent "Old Jim" like a trout rod. Lattie worked the boat around to give me a sideways pull and edged toward the fish so that I recovered most of my line but—"Whiew-w-w!" it went out again and I had another quarter of a mile of line to pump. When I brought the fish in this time he ran around the stern and forward on the other side. As I swung to follow him, the chair, which was too close to the gunwale, jammed my legs against it. My rod was almost against an awning post and I was in imminent danger of having it broken and of losing my tackle with my temper, which had already gone, when Hugh twisted me out of my predicament. After a while I got the fish alongside and Burt gave him the iron.

He was a Tiger, about the size of Hugh's Mackerel, probably three hundred and fifty pounds in weight, and this made possible an interesting comparison of their fights. They were both fully matured young males and were caught under similar conditions, one immediately after the other. The Mackerel Shark was unquestionably faster and he used speed and quick turning to better advantage than did the Tiger but I thought the Tiger was more powerful and more stubborn. Neither of them sounded. I should say that the Tiger was the harder to handle because with his mulishness he put the tackle to greater strain.

We were already learning that the Tiger Shark is a very difficult proposition—his very build and appearance show that. His fight is more like a determined infantry advance than like a cavalry dash. When the hook is set, he does not rush away with throttle open, in a wild frantic sprint. He just starts off fast and steady as though he is going somewhere and intends to keep going. The rodman's job is therefore not simply to humor the fish with exhausting runs on a long line but to wear him out by continuous resistance as stiff as the tackle will bear, and the angler's judgment as to what his tackle will bear decides whether he gets the shark or buys a new line (which, incidentally, costs about twenty dollars).

By this time, Hugh had cooled off and I was quite ready for some cocoanut milk, a cigarette, and a rest, so he took the chair. He promptly got a strike and hooked the fish which we recognized as a Mackerel Shark when he came up and went foaming along at the surface with fins and fluke in sight. After about an hour, Hugh

[94]

brought him to the gunwale, pretty thoroughly played out, and Burt did "his stuff."

During these fights the water about the boat was fairly "boiling" with sharks. At times there must have been a dozen in sight. The chum had, of course, attracted them but their curiosity was perfectly illustrated by their interest in the bright-colored float ball. Sometimes three or four would be nosing at it and pushing it about. Apparently they did not want to eat it and they did not even try to bite it—perhaps it was a game of water polo.

Following my usual practice, I had insisted that the sharks when brought in be slashed and hung overboard, tail up, to a stanchion. There the blood and oil from them was added to our chum-streak but late today, unfortunately, the lashings broke and three sharks floated away, followed by every one of the swarm which circled about us. Burt and Lattie insisted that this was because the dead sharks were a warning to the live ones who feared the same fate. I have heard other people say that same thing but it is not so. Just as the bleeding sharks are an attraction when tied to the boat so they are when they drift away with the tide and others follow to eat them as they came to them before.

Next day when we had to quit fishing there were sharks around the boat but they left and followed the carcasses when they were cast adrift. The boatmen then thought that, since sharks followed the carcasses to devour them, shark meat should be good bait so I humored them by allowing them to bait with shark steaks which, however, was entirely without success. It is only when there is semblance of recent life in the shark that others seem to wish to eat him. Mr. Schuetz later confirmed this by telling me that, in the Bahamas, he never baits his nets with shark flesh but uses skates, rays, or other fish.

[95]

The Ball at Mangrove Cay

This was the night of the ball. As we ran through the reef at Mangrove Cay, drums ashore were broadcasting notice of it and while we sat on deck, in the cool of the evening, enjoying a dinner of langouste, turtle steak and pawpaws, washed down with Planter's Punch, we could see a procession of natives moving along the beach toward the assembly while boatloads of singing men and women paddled along the shore.

If this were an ethnological treatise instead of a fishing story, a lot might be written about that ball where we met Andros society in strength, color and shades; where the populace assembled in its most festive mood, in its finest raiment and abandoned itself to the joy of being just natural, simple, careless people. What mattered it that tomorrow their shacks might be swept away by hurricane or their garden patches inundated by tidal wave? Tonight they were dancing.

It is almost unbelievable what toe-tickling rhythm that guitar, flute and tom-tom could produce and though at times it was almost like American jazz, at others it might have come straight from the Congo jungle. The "pair dancing" was modelled on that of so-called civilization but into it was introduced a sensuous African wiggle which even our most select night clubs might have shied at. Nevertheless, there was a dignity and a decorum which these simple people observed even in their abandonment to the joy of the dance.

Mangrove Cay was in holiday humor preparing for its coming annual festival. This festival requires a long time for preparation, a long time in progress, and a long time to run down afterward. Rehearsals were going on while we were there.

[96]

In a clearing, about a tall pole, beribboned like a Maypole, were clustered a swarm of half-naked children around whom sat cross-legged a circle of old women who pounded rhythmically on tom-toms. They and the children alternated in singing in a dialect, unintelligible to us, but they were evidently telling one another a most interesting story. All the time the children changed positions with different steps as though in a crude minuet. It was evidently all full of meaning but we did not understand it.

Aboard and on my transom after the ball, I dropped off to sleep thinking of those happy people—happy because their wants were so simple they need not worry. Their existence rolled along as our boat rides these smooth harbor waves with no immediate danger of swamping or capsizing. They seem never to consider what uncertainties the future may bring. Little disturbances are like the ripples slapping on our quarter—they just emphasize serenity—slap, sla-p, s-l-a-p.

THE PARTY
Hugh Wise, John Wise, Victor Coty,
Colonel Wise

THE CREW
Burt Bowe, Lattie Kemp

YOUNG LEOPARD SHARK
From painting by C. R. Knight
Courtesy of American Museum of Natural History

CHAPTER IX

OBSERVATIONS—MODIFICATIONS
MORE SHARKS

HAD I not already known it, these two days at Andros would have taught me the difficulty of fighting a big shark from an anchored boat. I had overlooked making provision for getting away after a strike without hoisting the anchor, and of course there was never time to hoist it. The boatmen, being new at the game, had not thought of any such thing and after each strike they fell over each other in confusion between wheel and cable. Burt was therefore sent ashore to get a keg or some other kind of buoy, and he returned with a small air tank from a discarded lifeboat. We rove the end of the anchor cable onto this tank and because of its resonance when it hit the water, it came to be known as the "gong," while the job of throwing it overboard was "kicking the gong around."

Before starting in the morning, I conducted a class to instruct the boatmen in their parts and soon had them coordinated in their various jobs.

I am convinced that the right way to fish for big sharks would be from the bow of a dory, towed stern foremost behind the motorboat and which could be cut loose when the shark is hooked. We lost several sharks, really our largest ones, by their breaking away before the big boat could get started or by their cutting the line on the keel of the slow turning boat.

I wanted to try this but, of course, a paddler was needed in the stern to steer the dory and neither Lattie nor Burt was keen for the job. Some day, when I have a boatman who has no more respect for a shark than I have, I will try it.

BIG WOOD CAY

When the sun's red disk peeped over the horizon where the "dawn comes up like thunder," we were foaming on our way toward Big Wood Cay for the preliminary bait-fishing. Barracuda were not as plentiful as they had been before but by noon we had enough bait, and dropped out to the channel for sharks. While we were still trolling for barracuda with light tackle, a small fifty-pound Tiger struck Hugh's bait and put up a lively fight before he was brought to gaff —another pretty little leopard.

Our first real shark this day was an eight-foot Tiger to me, and when Hugh relieved me in the chair he took another of about the same size. Both of these fish made fine fights, but they were not difficult because the crew was now working smoothly with us. At the rodman's shout: "STRIKE!" the gong banged overboard to be picked up later, and we were free to follow the shark.

As on the previous day, sharks were all around us, playing water polo with the float ball. Some of them were very large and we soon had Burt tossing the bait in their way. He "handed" Hugh's bait to a big fellow who took it in a swirl at the surface—"Kick the gong!" I yelled. "Over, Sir!" came the captain's reply. "Back her!" called Hugh as the shark started a grand run, dead astern. This was a big shark so I took post behind the chair to coach the helmsman, there was no time to turn, and at once came the order—"Full speed astern!"

[100]

Hugh squeezed hard down on the star-drag, pressed on the thumb-pad and the boat vibrated to the reversed engine but still the line kept jerking out—"Wha, wha, whee!" Three-fourths of it was off the spindle but the shark showed no signs of yielding—"Wha, wha, whee-e-e!" Twenty-five yards more and the brute would be free, but he turned! The boat, still going astern, began to turn and follow on an interior circle. Hugh's feet went onto the combing, his shoulders thrust back into the harness and he wound laboriously, recovering line. Then down went the shark, six fathoms to the bottom and a Princeton athlete could not pump him up. After a breathing spell, if that is what sharks get, away he went in another rush, outrunning the boat, now going full speed ahead. "Whee-e-e-e!" In less than two minutes the line recovered by Hugh was out again—the spindle came in sight—snap! It was all over! We had had several good views of this Tiger—more than twelve feet long —he was gone!

Hugh was ready for cocoanut milk now so I took the chair. Burt handed my bait to another big Tiger who came swishing along in company with a monster Hammerhead. Kemp swung the wheel in time to follow his first rush while I retarded the fish all I dared with drags and pad. I held him for a while and even imagined that he was beginning to turn when down he went and lay unyielding on the bottom. We chugged to right above him and saw him there in a nest of coral boulders. We steamed and drifted back and forth to pull him at different angles. Sometimes I lifted him a foot or two only to have him sink into another crevice. After an hour's struggle the inevitable happened—the line cut on a coral edge and that fight, too, was over.

"Burt," said I, "what sort of fish are you picking out for us?"

"They's the kind you wanted, ain't they? I told you we'd find 'em here."

I have no fisherman's alibi to offer. Hugh and I had been licked by those last two fish but it was hard fishing. The bottom here looked like the trenches and "boyeaux" on the Western Front and the fish, like the poilus, knew how to use them. In former experiences with sharks I had become accustomed to combatting their speed and power, and usually I could wear them out by getting them to turning on a long radius while the boat followed an inside circle on which its speed was sufficient to keep abreast of the fish. There had been nothing at the bottom but smooth sand, and, sooner or later, the shark could be made to leave that. Now we were up against a new problem, for the fish in deep crevices or among coral boulders could put *us* on the outside circle.

Usually sharks capture their prey by pursuit but here, with the water glass, we saw them lying behind turns of the coral labyrinth, awaiting their prey as pirates waited for merchant ships behind these islands in the days of Blackbeard.

TIGER TACTICS

Hugh, at the rod again, brought to iron another eight-foot Tiger, but later he shared my luck by hanging on to a big fellow who went down among the boulders and tore loose. As the bait left his mouth it was snapped up by a Wahoo (a species of large mackerel) who turned the line around a coral and cut it off.

A novel interest in this fishing in the Bahamas was that we could see through the clear water what was happening at the other end of the line, sometimes five or six fathoms away. But also we confronted difficulties resulting from the irregular bottom; the fish could change the fight from long-range sparring to short-arm infighting and this added greatly to the strain on the tackle. Often the shark would not run and his energy had to be sapped from him by back-breaking pumping. Again, he might go off like a speedboat, or worse, like a steady irresistible submarine.

These Tigers, with which I had hitherto had no experience, showed not only the stubbornness of Duskies, but, at times, almost the speed of Mackerel Sharks and they were more powerful than either. Therefore I abandoned my pet "tapered line," and notwith-standing strong predilection for light tackle, I found myself forced to the conclusion that a 12/0 real with No. 36 line would have been better than our 9/0 and No. 30.

All this makes me more than ever realize how risky it is for a man to attempt the formulation of rules for either tackle or methods. In fishing for heavy sharks there certainly are general principles to be followed but rigid rules will result in many lost fish and much broken tackle.

However:

> There is a rule in life
> And it applies to you—
> On one end you wear your bonnet,
> On the other end, your shoe.
> Be sure you use your bonnet end
> In everything you do.
> Use your bonnet end!—*Anonymous*.

THE CAMERAMAN'S VIEW

While Hugh and I were so intent upon our angling and the crew

[103]

were sweating at their work, there was an even busier man aboard. Victor Coty is essentially a fisherman and he is one of the best-known dry-fly men on our eastern streams. On this trip, however, he consistently refused to take the chair or be anything but a thoroughly fascinated cameraman. Hugh and I, working in the cockpit, often entirely forgot Vic until we heard him scrambling about on top of the awning or saw him shinning down a stanchion. Once, as he braced himself against a narrow awning frame, I called to him: "If you slip off there and splash into that swarm of excited sharks we will have to get a rebate on your return ticket to America." When he came down that evening he said: "Boy, that was an experience! It is one thing to say airily, 'there were dozens of sharks around us,' but it is a very different matter to look at them from up there. Why, you can look away down into the water and see one sinister graceful form after another glide in from nowhere and join the column circling the boat and I know what would happen to a fellow if he lost his toe-hold on that crazily rocking awning—he would just be shark food, that's all! One big Tiger had a hungry look in his eyes every time he came around and glared up at me. Some of them were so large that I wondered if they could not overturn the boat. Picture yourself perched up there above those floating demons with only the little awning frame to stop your slide into their snapping jaws! 'STRIKE!' yells the rodman—'Bang!' goes the cable overboard. 'Free, Sir!' calls the helmsman and the reel shrieks and the boat trembles with engine throttle open. Then come staccato orders: 'Follow him!—Full speed ahead!—Full speed astern!—Ahead!—Half speed—Back her!' and the engine roars and the awning sways. This keeps up for hours with agonizing moments when, in spite of a ninety-pound drag and the speed of the boat, the fish rips

[104]

out fathoms of line, and with moments of relief when the lost line is slowly recovered. Finally, I hear, 'Ready with the iron!—Let him have it!' and, hanging over the awning edge, I point the camera at Burt who throws the dart. It strikes home—it holds—the rodman throws his free spindle lever and slumps in the chair! The lanyard whirls from the bucket and then strong arms haul in the Tiger for the lance when his snapping jaws appear at the gunwale. This is what I saw and what I heard up there. What amazing vitality these Tigers have—what fighting fools they are!

"Tiger shooting with a rifle from an elephant's back may be exciting, but that it is more exciting than Tiger shooting with a camera from the top deck of a crazily rolling boat, well, you will have to show me."

In this description, Victor lets his fishing enthusiasm run free, but on the whole trip he never allowed it to make him forget his camera and his wonderful pictures show that.

In the beginning I was skeptical about being bothered by a photographer milling around, but we never were bothered by Coty. He never demanded that we pose for him nor that we do anything but handle our fish in sportsmanlike and natural manner. That is why his pictures are so good. I saw them shown in a New York lecture hall today, more than a year after they were taken. They gave me the thrill I had had when catching the sharks; I felt the bound of the boat, I smelled the salt spray. I caught those sharks over again today, and when the lecture ended I was all "het up" and wanted cocoanut milk.

CHAPTER X

SHARK LORE—YARNS—NATURE FAKES

JUNE 23 we had to run back to Nassau for ice and supplies, and a good night's rest in a comfortable bed would not be unacceptable. Also, I had picked up considerable native lore which I wished to discuss with men in whose opinions I had confidence.

SETTING HIS SKIN

One such notion was that a Nurse Shark, when attacked, could tighten his hide to resist the harpoon. Natives generally believed this, as also did the British Commissioner who thought it might be the origin of the native expression, "setting his skin," by which they imply a man's "preparation to resist." Mr. Schuetz, Captain Brown, and the crews of the shark-fishing tugs of the National Fisheries Corporation all confirmed this and were willing to be so quoted.

Other sharks, too, may have this same capacity and experiments proved to me that a harpoon which would bounce from the hide of a live shark, as from a steel plate, could be easily driven into it when the fish was dead.

The next year, Schuetz, on the basis of experiments and observations made by him, offered the following explanation: In the hide of a Nurse Shark, the denticles are set somewhat like hexagonal tiles in a bathroom floor, the tissue between them being like the cement between the tiles. When agitated or touched, the shark voluntarily or by a reflex action draws these "tiles" together so that even a harpoon point or a knife edge does not penetrate between them, thus "setting his skin" into a continuous sheet of resistant armor plate.

FIGHTS BETWEEN MAN AND SHARK

I especially wished to check up on those lurid yarns about fights between man and shark in the shark's element—water.

There are reliable accounts of swimmers who have rescued others by frightening away the shark, such, for example, as the heroic saving of a man in Australia for which the rescuer was decorated by the King. Personally I have never believed that a man swimming could successfully fight a big shark with a knife. To drive a knife through the denticled hide would require great power, and there would be small chance of its reaching one of the two vital and well-protected spots, heart or brain, even though the shark remained passive during the operation. Meantime, one slash with his teeth or one wallop with his tail would end the fight.

During our inquiries in the Bahamas we heard how a movie company, having failed to find any man who was willing to dive after a live shark with a knife, used for the picture a dead shark which was operated by fine wires.

In another picture, the shark for the combat was caught the day before and tethered to a buoy so he would be tired out. In the morning his mouth was sewed up with wire and he was anchored fore and aft to a large iron cart-wheel tire. Then the courageous (?) diver went down and dispatched him with a spear while the camera clicked. The fellow who told me this story admitted that he was the diver, and assured me he had to have the spear shiny so it would photograph well. "Could you have killed the shark," I asked, "if he had not been tired out and if his mouth had not been sewed up?"—"Hell, no!" he replied. "And damned if I'd try it either!"

DIVER AND OCTOPUS

There was another famous movie made in the Bahamas in which a death-struggle between a diver and a huge octopus was shown. The terrible monster enfolded the diver in his powerful tentacles and would have crushed him but for the diver's trusty knife! I learned from the diver himself how he so miraculously escaped. The octopus, parts of which may still be seen in Nassau, was made of painted canvas. In his tentacles were springs which were extended when the octopus was pumped full of air, but when pumping ceased, the tentacles contracted about the man. This was an ingenious mechanical device but one hardly calculated to convey zoological information.

Some of my readers may have seen a movie picturing a terrific battle between a gigantic octopus and a huge shark. In nature, such a fight could not last long, but in the picture it did. A small octopus was tied to a little Dog Shark by a fine wire so that their frantic struggles to pull apart seemed to be a fight to the death between contestants, magnified into monsters by the camera set close to the tank.

As a matter of fact, octopi are rather inoffensive creatures, crawling slowly around over the bottom in search of crustaceans which are their principal food, and their apparently dreadful arms with many suckers are used to enfold and turn over rocks to get at that food. They are very much smaller than fiction would have us believe and ten feet across would be a big one.

I can learn of no credible report of an attack on man by this

[109]

creature nor can I find an instance of such in all the scientific literature dealing with octopi. In Hawaii, where the octopus is a delicacy,
the natives dive barehanded for him and drag him from his hiding
places under the coral.

Swordfish and Whale

I recently saw a movie picturing a battle between a swordfish
and a whale. The swordfish was leaping high in the air, apparently
lunging furiously at the whale, while the audience chorused "Oh!"
Looking critically at the whale, however, he seemed to be dead and
I thought a line was dangling from the mouth of the swordfish. I
even thought that the swordfish was struggling to avoid being
dragged against the whale as well he might for had he driven his
sword into the whale's thick blubber, he probably could not have
pulled it out, or it might have been broken off as it is when he happens to ram it into a boat. The audience was immensely pleased and
that was the purpose of the picture.

Dr. C. H. Townsend, Director of the New York Aquarium, has
checked up on a large number of stories of such fights, but he concluded that there was nothing to them and he thinks that perhaps
they have grown out of observations of attacks upon whales by a
smaller variety of toothed whales, *Orca gladiator*. We find among
the grandfathers of modern fish yarns tales of how the "shark whip-
peth the whale on the surface while the swordfish speareth him
from beneath."—A rather efficient "ganging-up" on poor old
whale, I should call it, but what a pity that modern educational films
should be allowed to deceive the public by such nature-faking.

True Shark Attacks and Yarns

Though I have minimized probability of danger from shark attacks, yet I recognize that there are many well-authenticated instances in which sharks have attacked men and even boats.

Doctor Gudger has told me how at Key West his boat was attacked by a large wounded Tiger Shark who splintered the boat stem with his strong teeth. Doctor C. F. Holder, in his book, relates similar experiences at Tortugas. Of course reports of such scientists are incontrovertible.

Mr. E. M. Schuetz has recorded his personal experiences in his diary, from which he allows me to quote these instances.

In May, 1934, in the Berry Islands, a large Tiger Shark, wounded by a harpoon, turned upon a ten-foot dory, seized its bow in his jaws and shook the boat so violently that its three occupants were thrown into its bottom. "We were like ice in a cocktail shaker," said Schuetz. Such an experience, however, does not seem to have chilled Schuetz' enthusiasm for shark-hunting nor to have unsteadied his aim with the harpoon.

In June, 1933, at Gorda Cay, a Mackerel Shark which Schuetz was chasing, turned upon the dinghy and left some of his teeth in the keel. In the same month, a Yellow Shark, missed with the harpoon, seized the shaft in his teeth and bit it into three pieces.

To my mind, these incidents do not indicate aggressiveness on the part of the sharks, but rather retaliation to attacks.

One of the most exciting experiences related to me by Schuetz was that of a large shark, who, when hooked on a hand-line, seized the rudder and then the propeller of the boat which he might have capsized had he not been cut loose.

[111]

Another of Schuetz' accounts seems to show not only the viciousness of a shark but also some degree of intelligence. While Schuetz was casting from a ledge, a large shark tried to swipe him off with its tail. Schuetz, dodging the tail, quit fishing and clambered up from the ledge, which shows that Schuetz had reasoning power.[1]

At Nassau the following story was widely circulated and I was able to interrogate several witnesses. Six men had been recently drowned from a capsized boat. The bodies lay at the bottom while sharks circled around but did not disturb them. When, however, the bodies began to be raised with grappling-hooks the sharks dashed in and tore them to pieces. It would seem that the semblance of life which movement gave them attracted the sharks.

The discussion of all this with experienced fishermen in Nassau led naturally to the old question of what a man should do if he found himself in the water with sharks nearby. All of us agreed that he should kick, splash, yell, and raise all possible commotion but none of us would wish to be held responsible for giving such advice. Frankly, I should be willing to let the shark have the swimming hole, and I would raise no question of riparian privilege.

The foregoing stories, received firsthand from men whose training and experience eliminate probability of excited exaggeration or hasty conclusions, can be taken as bases for deduction. There are other stories, however, in which, from facts truthfully told, deductions may have been hastily made. For example:

The Clyde liner "Una" sank, November, 1918, in the British

1. Further consideration of this incident, however, leads Schuetz to believe that the shark was really not swiping at him but simply swung his tail out of water with a sudden turn when he was frightened by another man on the bank. What a pity to spoil such a good story!

West Indies. The vessel went down in a comparatively smooth sea but there was not room in her lifeboats for her crew and the seventy-five negro laborers who were passengers. Many had to take to extemporized rafts. Swarms of sharks surrounded these, seizing and tearing to pieces men who slipped from the overloaded and topply floats. So far the story as published is well authenticated, but that the sharks were actually trying to get aboard the rafts or to get under them and overturn them with their backs, as the story goes on to relate, seems less likely than that they simply collided with them, excited by the blood in the water, without intending to capsize them.

In *Copeia*, May, 1919, to which I have previously referred, Mr. Coles tells of an adventure which may possibly be another instance of doubtful conclusions from correct premises. Says he:

"In 1903, in the Bight of Cape Lookout, North Carolina, I was out in a very small skiff harpooning turtles, and armed with rifle, light harpoon, and heavy knife, when an eighteen-foot shark, easily recognizable as this species (White Shark), charged, halting only when in contact with my skiff, where, with its large staring eye watching my every move, it lay for some seconds almost motionless with part of its back exposed above the surface, while I crouched with finger on the trigger of the high-powered rifle, aimed in front of the first dorsal fin. The shark then began a series of rapid evolutions, turning several times on its back while circling the skiff, into which it splashed much water. It then retired to a distance approximating a hundred yards and then, turning, charged at great speed directly at the skiff, when suddenly in the line of its attack a large logger-head turtle came to the surface and was seized in the jaws of the shark, which I heard crushing through the shell of the turtle. I am convinced that this shark had satisfied himself that I was suitable

[113]

for food and had only retired to acquire speed for leaping into the skiff and seizing me, and that the coming to the surface of the turtle at that instant was all that saved me from a dangerous, knife to shagreen fight."

Now, was that shark after the man in the boat or was he after the turtles in and around it?

Quite different from these stories are the yarns of "The Oldest Inhabitant," "The Pioneer of the Community," and, particularly, "The Weather-Beaten Sea-Farer." These yarns are often without foundation and make one wonder whether the narrator or the listener is the more gullible.

Fishing yarns have a way of growing with age, so a man may be justified in questioning even the oldest recorded of them. Was Jonah swallowed by a whale, or did he merely see a whale, or did he just think he saw one after a night ashore?

A remarkable story, vouched for by the Secretary of the Institute of Jamaica and for which there seems to be documentary evidence, is that, in the 18th century the American privateer "Nancy" was seized by H. M. S. "Sparrow" in the Caribbean Sea and her captain was taken to Port Royal for trial. Because of lack of evidence against him, the captain was about to be acquitted when the commander of H. M. S. "Abergavenny" came in with the ship's papers of the "Nancy" which had been thrown overboard but which the commander of the "Abergavenny" had taken from the stomach of a shark caught off the coast of Haiti. On the evidence in these papers the captain of the "Nancy" was convicted. These papers, known as the "shark's papers" were put on exhibition in the Institute of Jamaica where it is said they may still be seen.[2]

2. Brooklyn Museum of Science Bulletin, Vol. III, No. 1.

In the Bahamas there is a dearth of picturesque stories and superstitions such as are common among the more fanciful Hawaiians. In Hawaii shark sagas have become a sort of crude mythology, still accepted by some of the older people. In this mythology there were shark gods, sharks which changed form to humans, to animals, and to birds; sharks which guarded the riparian rights of certain people, sharks which piloted the war canoes of tribes.

In Pearl Harbor there remained, until destroyed by the dredging for the Naval Base, a circular enclosure of coral boulders, known as "The Shark Pen." According to tradition this was the scene of gladiatorial contests between men and sharks during fêtes of ancient rulers.

None of the weird tales I heard in Hawaii quite equals one told in Sheldon's *Reminiscences of Hawaii*, how two sailors, who deserted their ship and jumped overboard, mounted astride a friendly shark, and, guiding him by pats on the nose, rode to shore, meantime regaling themselves on Remoras plucked from the shark's hide.

It was interesting to hear in the Bahamas a superstition which is common in Hawaii, in Cuba, and at home: that when a swimmer comes unexpectedly into a warm streak, it is the path of a shark and he should get out. If he believes that he probably will want to get out.

SHARK AND REMORA

CHAPTER XI

BIOLOGY AND MORE SHARKS

WE got a late start from Nassau on the morning of June 24, because it was the birthday of the Prince of Wales. That made it almost impossible to get a Nassauvian to work or even to bring us supplies—holiday is holiday in Nassau. When we finally did get off we ran to West End Bay, on New Providence Island, but we had saved time by purchasing bait in Nassau.

John, our biologist, had been staying at the hotel with his mother and studying bird life about Nassau, but he now joined us with his silk seines and formaldehyde. During the remainder of the trip he was fully occupied with these, except when the progress of a shark fight made any other activity on the boat impossible. A large order had devolved upon John, because we were depending upon him to collect certain shark parasites and other invertebrate specimens for Professor Dahlgren and we really did not give John a fair chance. The rodmen were not inclined to yield the cockpit for biological research, the cameraman took slight interest in things too small to be photographed, and dissection of bloody sharks on the clean decks did not appeal to the captain nor did he show enthusiasm for the hauling of shagreen hides over the varnished gunwales. Nevertheless, John did splendid work collecting specimens and he got Schuetz interested enough to continue their collection after our departure.

PARASITES, REMORAS AND PILOT FISH

The subject of shark parasites is much too large a one to discuss extensively here. Most sharks are infested with them. They bore through the hide, burrow in the nostrils, enter the intestines and utilize, generally, all other available choice spots from which they may draw sustenance.

Quite different from parasites are Remoras, small fish attaching themselves to "dead head" their travel and to profit by scraps of the shark's food but not actually preying upon his body. They are simply marine "hitchhikers" and "panhandlers."

Little is known of the ancestry of Remoras. There is nothing else like them in the sea, where they are still a mystery. One species clings to sharks far out on the ocean, one is found on the gills of swordfish and another on whales. All of these may be loosely called Remoras but the one most familiar to shark fishers is the graceful, slender little Shark Sucker Fish, about fifteen inches long. He is beautifully colored in grey, green and black and has bold longitudinal stripes of black and white along his sides but, chameleonlike, he can change into a dull uniform grey to match the shark carrying him. His head, flattened and elliptical on top, is equipped with slats like the shutters of a Venetian window blind and with this apparatus he is able to adhere to the body of his host. Usually these little Sucker Fish are seen swimming around sharks or clinging to them, and they often hold on until the shark is hoisted aboard. But they also live independent lives and being voracious feeders, they are not infrequently caught on the hook. Being so often found in the company of the shark, the Sucker Fish is often erroneously called Pilot Fish.

The true Pilot Fish, a small black-banded relative of the Amberjack, accompanies the shark as do several other species but he does not attach or "hang on" as do Remoras. He, too, may profit by

[118]

scraps of the shark's food, but the real reason for this strange companionship with a monster who to most of the finny world is a menace and a terror seems to be his desire for "security." Much superstitious lore is associated with the Pilot Fish, as for instance the belief that they guide the shark to food or away from danger, but there is no scientific foundation for such stories.

Dearth and vagueness of scientific knowledge in regard to the Remora family should make us admit our ignorance but, in addition, fanciful tales serve to confuse even the little we know. Pliny's "Shipholder," probably a slender little Sucker Fish, was credited with being able to hold on to a ship and stop it. Other old writers, who should have known better, have told how this little fish interfered with navigation and even ascribe to it important rôles in naval engagements.

Rabelais, whom we must suspect of talking with his tongue in his cheek, tells how the Remora obstructed commerce: "This silly weakly fish," says he, "in spite of all the winds that blow from the thirty-two points of the compass, will in the midst of a hurricane make you the biggest first-rater remain stock still, as if she were becalmed, or the blustering tribe had blown their last." But, not content with that one, Rabelais tells how useful the Remora was in the recovery of gold: "With the flesh of that fish, preserved with salt, you may fish gold out of the deepest well that was ever sounded with a plummet; for it will certainly draw up the precious metal."

How unfortunate for me that this art was lost before I became interested in sharks and Remoras! I have never found gold sticking on a Remora. Can this be because our gold is now safely impounded in the United States Treasury, or because the Remora is afraid to be caught with gold in his possession?

[119]

BACK TO ANDROS

Having had no luck with sharks at West End we hoisted anchor and put out for Andros. Hardly had we cleared the bay before we ran into a fierce little rain squall and in spite of the delay it caused us, it was fascinating. The wind howled and sheets of rain swashed under the awnings; about us all was leaden grey; not far off golden sunlight danced on the water and, in the distance, the land was splotched with black shadows on emerald green. We held our powerful little boat head on till the squall blew over and then sped on to High Cay where we anchored for the night on a gently rolling sea.

"Here's where we get 'em tomorrow?" I asked Burt. "Yessuh, I guarantee it." "Well, I suppose you are entitled to a Bahama pirate prize. How would you like a rich wife?" "Nosuh, I don't want no woman to take care of."

Burt was feeling rather low. On shore an insect had bitten him, his leg was swollen and he was sick all over. He lay below inert and very quiet until suddenly he asked, "Kunnel, what do you think of this life after death business?" "Burt," I replied, "those golden stairs would be hard for you to climb with that lame leg—better not die."

In Nassau I had tried to get an electric light bulb on a waterproof cable to connect with the boat's circuit and to be put overboard. The Prince of Wales having prevented this, I contrived an apparatus with the water glass and an electric torch and with it spent part of the night in observation. The light attracted fish and, though the apparatus was none too satisfactory, I did see some interesting things before a barracuda, leaping at the light, nearly caught my hand and forced me to abandon the contraption.

For John and me the remainder of the night was literally "rot-ten," and in the morning we discovered that we had been trying to sleep with our heads over the fish-box where we still had some of our Nassau bait, no longer pristine in freshness.

ANDROS AND BIG SHARKS

At sunrise we went to bait fishing with handlines, horsing the fish in so quickly, that we got after the sharks early. Hugh started in the chair and his bait was hardly out before a huge Tiger came churning through the chum streak and dove for it. Away he went, fins above the water, throwing jets of spray forward and leaving behind a trail of foam—a long fast rush. Kemp danced his boat around and let Hugh recover line. "You've got him licked!" I yelled,—too soon for with a great surge the shark went off on another run, took the line to the end and parted it at the double. That was a big fish—too powerful to be held by any angler's tackle from the big boat. He might have been saved, fishing in a dory.

Now I took the chair and soon was hung onto another Tiger and fought with him till I had him within fifty feet of the boat. We saw that fellow several times and knew that he was easily a five hundred pounder but he was not making the fight he could have made. After his preliminary rush he yielded readily to my pumping and then alternately followed in unresisting, or brought the line "solid." When we got a close view this peculiar performance was explained. He was a "roller." He would lie alongside the leader and move along with it, then, in a swirl of water, he would turn across the wire and roll it several times around him. Lying broadside to my pull he could not be budged until my pumping unwound him. Again and again this was repeated. Four turns of the leader around his thick body would bring the line against his rough hide and he seemed to be trying to do just that. Finally he succeeded, and "Snap!"—he was gone with two dollars' worth of hook, swivels and leader hanging from his ugly jaws.

This was the first time I ever actually watched the performance of this trick but I am satisfied that it has been played on me many times. Once before this I saw a shark suddenly cease pulling, run under the line and sandpaper it in twain with his denticled hide. Unquestionably, too, sharks do sometimes reach the line with their teeth but more often, I believe, they cut loose with the rough hide of their fins or bodies.

OUR BIGGEST SHARK

We returned to the anchor, picked up the gong, Burt laid a new slick and Hugh floated out a fresh barracuda. "Wha-a-a" went the reel, with that bass note which means a slow run, and then the fish turned and swam leisurely toward the boat. He did not seem to know that he was hooked or if he did know it he was not in the least perturbed. When we saw him, the hook in his mouth, and saw what a big fellow he was, I yelled for the gong to go over and with Kemp's "Over, Sir!" the shark woke up and gave us a grand run followed by an hour of forward, back, starboard, port, while Hugh pumped and sweated. When the double came up the fight was nowhere near over for, with another surge, out went three hundred yards of line to be pumped back only to go again. When after several such runs he was brought to the surface a hundred feet away, the shark changed tactics and began surging in small circles, diving and looping underwater and twice he went over backwards, rolling as he

WHAT MAKES A REEL HOT
The Colonel's line sizzles out.

THE BIOLOGIST AT WORK

OUR FINEST SHARK
Length 11′ 7″. Girth 74.1″
Weight 954 lbs.

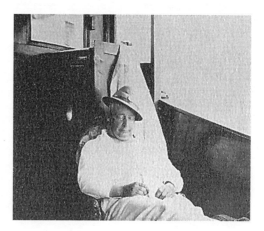

THE END OF
A PERFECT WEEK

looped, like an airplane in an Immelmann turn—all in plain sight and to the accompaniment of a shrieking reel. What a fight! But Hugh was master of it and finally the shark committed the tactical error of swimming too close to Burt's poised dart which flew out and struck into the gills. A rush to the end of the lanyard, now leaving a pink trail behind him, and the shark was hauled in for the *coup de grâce*—vitality and power conquered by a tenth of its strength, now slumped in the chair.

This Great Blue was the finest shark of our expedition and he deserves record of his measurements in this, his obituary: length, 11 feet, 7 inches, girth, 6 feet, 2 inches, weight, 954 pounds.

We Have to Quit

Our bait was gone now so we went back and raided the barracudas at Fresh Creek Channel, returning later to the shark grounds. Seeing sharks as soon as the chum went out had gotten to be a habit with us and they were all around before our baits were floated to them. A big Tiger nailed mine, when it splashed into the water. He was a monster fully fourteen feet long. We were ready for him, the gong went over, Kemp jerked open the throttle and we were following. But his speed was greater than the speed of the boat and I had to keep slipping line. When the spindle showed, nothing could be done but hope that the line might hold. It did hold for a little while and then came that sick feeling at the pit of the stomach when it broke. The rod snapped up straight, the line whipped out of the water and I fell against the chair back—licked! I admit it, next year we have got to use heavier tackle! But, oh, if I had been in a dory!—what a ride!

Squalls were appearing all about us, it was several hours past noon and we were sixty miles from Nassau where we had to be in the morning to sail home. We could not stay for even one more shark, so, with aching hearts we took up anchor and waved farewell to Andros Island and to its waters still boiling with sharks.

What a grand four days we had had—three or four big sharks each day and licked by larger ones than we had caught! We had found the lair of the Tiger and we are going back to fight it out with him as soon as we can.

The engine purred, we were under way; a big fin came up in our wake, but it was a challenge we could not accept. The next day, on the Munson liner, steaming away from Bahama waters, I gazed regretfully back, still thinking of the droves of my friends, the enemy, we were leaving there. Dozing in my deck chair, I saw dark graceful forms slithering through crystal depths, I heard the big reel whine, I felt the stout rod bend and the leather harness bear down on my shoulders. It was the end of a perfect week.

CHAPTER XII

PREPARING—THINKING—MULLING

WHEN we returned from the Bahamas, Hugh and I brought with us memories of a wonderful week of sport and the experience of some exciting shark fights, but John had a collection of shark jaws, ray tails, leeches, Remoras, jellyfish and parasites which delighted Doctor Dahlgren. Among his "Fifty-Seven Varieties" of pickled invertebrates there was a jar containing some inconsequential looking little bugs, and this was the one upon which Dahlgren enthusiastically pounced, for he immediately saw how important those little *copepods* might be to science. To Hugh and me they were just the feathers from Old Harry's angels' wings but Dahlgren, after petting them himself, sent them to the world authority, Professor Charles B. Wilson, at the Oceanographic Institution and that eminent scientist wrote me:

I have incorporated what I learned from them in a paper now being published. . . . I cannot do better than to quote what I have there written: . . . "Eighty years ago, Professor J. D. Dana of Yale University made some male copepods the types of a new genus and species which he named *Specilligus curticaudis,* but he found no females to complete his species and none have been taken since then although similar males have been often captured." It has been generally agreed that his specimens were not new but were really the males of some species already described. But there has been a constant dispute as to where they should be placed. There were some of these males in the Tortugas specimens which I was describing and, at the very time I was endeavoring to locate them, there came one of those opportune coincidences that occasionally surprise even the most prosaic investigator—I received from Doctor Dahlgren a vial containing the specimens you had sent him and, behold, the question of eighty years duration as to identity was solved as soon as I had a good look at them. They proved to be two young females and seven males of a shark parasite known long before Dana described his species. . . . The seven formed a perfect series so there could no longer be any question as to identity. I am greatly obliged to you for solving the dilemma. . . .

I must here confess frankly that when I received that letter I did not know exactly what copepods were and had to dig out books and study to learn that they are small parasites and hosts for other parasites and that directly and indirectly they provide food for other marine creatures, including the whale. Beyond getting up our fishing trip, I had no more to do with finding those copepods, and so with disrupting Dana's theory, than I had to do with the discovery of the rings of Saturn—John captured them and Dahlgren recognized them as worth having. Thank heaven, I did not chuck them out of the porthole! Nevertheless, this may be taken as a striking instance of what I said as to the importance of turning over to scientists unusual specimens, even when and especially when you do not know what they are.

ANGLER NOTIONS

I had brought home with me, too, a head full of ideas, good, bad and indifferent, about improvement in tackle and I spent hours tinkering at refinements which after all were not essential because I could catch all the sharks I really *needed* on my old stuff. But that is part of the game!

When the boy who wants beefsteak and potatoes, and wants lots of them, becomes man and epicure, he hankers after canvasback and burgundy, but he is less concerned about quantity than with preparation and service. That same boy may have had fun catching trout on a pole, cut with a jackknife by the brookside, and probably he measured his fun by the length of his string of fish; but since he graduated into the dry-fly class, he uses a three-ounce split-bamboo for his sport and what counts is not the number of his trout but the aesthetic manner of taking them.

I doubt that I shall ever again have such fun killing sharks with sportsman-like tackle, as I had when a boy with my rope and dog chain, but that would not satisfy me now because, unfortunately I have advanced into the class where method, not results, makes the sport. The fish is of little value anyway, the thrill is in the matching of skill against power—in winning the fight against a quarry who has a chance.

I wish to see the fish dash in

And upon the dainty morsel
Snaps his jaws in savage rapture
But the line so sudden tightens
That he feels the hooks—and writhing,
Mad he turns and plunges wildly.

I want even an outlaw shark to have a fair fight. I want to see him run and jump and loop. I want him on a slender line and a flexible rod, slipping him out and winding him back until he is whipped to the point when the boatman can take the leader and bring him to iron. So, while I sit working with pliers and soldering iron, I seem to be trying to assemble a tackle with which I can win if I am expert, but with which I shall lose if I am not skillful. I put on a hook to hold a properly handled thousand-pounder but an awkwardly managed fish of a fourth that weight would straighten it out. The little bronze chain will resist shark teeth but it is not irresistibly strong. The wire leader, though it would not lift the weight of the fish, will, with the spring of a cleverly handled flexible rod withstand his most violent surges.

This all seems very artificial, but is that not exactly what sport angling is? We make a difficult game of it so we may win only by skill and the pleasure of the game is in the exercise of the skill.

Also, it is to be remembered that no inconsiderable part of the pleasure of fishing is in the preparation for it. Sitting in our studies we assemble tackle which we could probably get better ready-made at a tackle shop. When, however, we splice the hook on a leader we feel at least one fish strain at it or we picture to ourselves the bending rod while we wrap on its guides. This fishing business must be regarded as primarily fun, and it is not to be taken as solemnly as some of us devotees would seem to consider it. One of the best anglers I ever knew was a one-legged inmate of the Virginia lunatic asylum. Then, too, the pleasure may be largely or entirely imaginary. The frost-encrusted window panes of my room may become the spray-coated port lights of "The Bessie"; the billowing snow drifts outside can change into foaming green waves; wintry blasts may sound like breezes murmuring through the rigging. Burt comes with the chum-bucket—no, it is not Burt, it is the maid with the tea tray.

Coming one day from my experimenting with tackle, I happened to mention to another deep-sea angler what I had been doing. "What!" he exclaimed. "Making tackle to take sharks! For heaven's sake make some that sharks won't take. The damned things take all of mine. They monopolize the ocean!" "Exactly," I replied, "and if you can't get away from them, have fun with them—'don't cuss the trusts, get into them.' "

[128]

PREPARING—THINKING—MULLING

A Homemade Tackle

All this talk about making tackle brings back to mind the first I ever made. It was in the Philippines and was not to take sharks but a shark took it. My battalion was at a God-forsaken little coast town, resting up after an arduous campaign preparatory to another. The shores about such a village are always covered with nets and weirs for a large component of the Filipino's diet is fish and at their sea-coast villages hauls of fine varieties are tremendous. The Filipino, however, prefers the smaller kinds, which he salts and dries in the sun, but, above all he liked our commissary issue of canned salmon— "Gold Fish" the soldiers called it and they cordially detested it. Congress, with paternal eye on our infant Alaskan industry, required that canned salmon be a part of the army ration but mess sergeants, believe it or not, were able to trade it with the natives, one pound for ten pounds of fresh pompano, mackerel or the like.

Interesting though it was to watch the natives trap and net fish and to see their marvelous swimming and diving amongst their "corrales," yet it was not sport for the inveterate angler. Nor could the hauling in of a big game-fish on hand-line appease the sportsman's yearning to feel the tug on light line and slender rod. There was, however, neither that sort of line nor that sort of rod where we were, and Manila, with which we had only monthly communication, was probably the nearest place where anyone had ever heard of a reel. Clearly, if I wanted sporty tackle I would have to make it for myself, and that is what I set about doing.

Finding a clever native bamboo worker, I persuaded him, or, rather, coerced him, into the building of a rod under my direction. From the beginning this was difficult because the native thought it

[129]

was utter nonsense to construct a pole when so many fine straight bamboos were growing all around us. These he insisted were longer and stronger than any pole we could make and in that he was doubtless correct. Nevertheless, we selected proper male canes, split them into strips, tested them, and fashioned them into wedge-shaped cross-section. Then we glued them together and wrapped them with blue silk thread, laboriously ravelled from the seams of a pair of full-dress trousers. The cork grip was made from an old life preserver; guides, of brass wire letter clips; tip-top, hammered from a copper penny. The aluminum shaving brush tube from my dressing case made an excellent reel-seat. Meantime a native jeweller cleverly constructed a reel whose plates were silver pesos and the spindle a piece of brass cleaning rod. A Chinese weaver spun a line of fine strands of Manila hemp and waterproofed it with native gum. Now, laugh if you like, but I had a splendid one-piece, seven-foot, light sea-rod and a tackle as good for sport as vom Hofe's best.

In a canoe along the shore and up the river, I spent many happy hours with this outfit while my men were resting, and my catches were large and varied. At first, my native paddler was bewildered and rather disgusted. He saw no sense in allowing a fish to run off just to be wound back again and he argued that if the Commandante would use a stronger line and a stouter pole he could catch a fish much quicker and then catch another. Soon, however, Juan came to appreciate the game and occasionally when I crawled under the matting "tapanca" to rest from the sun, I let him use the tackle. He finally became angler enough even to lie about his catches and one day I heard him telling about catching a fifty-pound *dorado* which actually weighed less than twenty.

After a few weeks this sport came to a sudden end, when a fish which I was playing was seized by a tiburone. Before I could cut the line, "Crack!" went the rod, leaving me with only the butt in my hand. There was not time to build another rod before we again took to the mountains and jungles, but there was ample consolation in the fact that the labor of making it had been many times repaid by the sport I had had with the rod and one cannot measure sport by cost.

I seem to have gotten off the track for I promised to confine this book to sharks but after all it was a shark which wrecked my rod.

A Shark Attack

At this place occurred the only shark attack which has ever come under my personal observation. One of the fish pounds had been torn loose at the bottom from the supporting poles and a number of canoes clustered about it for repair work. The first native to go down, taking rattan withes in his teeth, dove in. Hardly had he disappeared when there was a swirl below and he popped to the surface followed by a huge shark which whirled and dashed away. Amid great noise and confusion the man was hauled into a canoe. His loincloth had been ripped from him and on his thigh were two ugly crescent-shaped lacerations from shark teeth.

My explanation of this incident is that while the shark lay at the opening in the pound, the diver plunged almost onto him and that the surprised shark whirled and seized the man. Having tasted blood, the shark might have been expected to finish the diver but, following him to the surface, he was frightened away by the commotion in the canoes. Be that as it may, the bitten man gave up fishing and thenceforth took employment on a copra plantation where, in the tops of cocoanut-palms, he probably felt safe from sharks.

[131]

Between Seasons at Princeton

During the winter of 1934–1935, when the water was too cold for sharks and too rough for me to go after them, I spent a lot of time floundering in a poorly charted sea of shark literature. Taxonomy I found rather thoroughly treated but the characteristics and habits of the fish were very sketchily passed over. It was easy to learn that in certain species "the palato-quadrate apparatus does not articulate with the cranium," but where and how would you go after a Tiger Shark? "The *Isurus dekayi* has erect pupils," but will a Mackerel Shark attack man? Why is he not a game-fish while his cousin, the "Mako," is? What I am trying to get into this book is information for a fisherman, and I must not allow Samuel Garman to take too much space from Isaac Walton. Sam has to tell Ike something about what he is catching but he must not hog too much of the cockpit. Fully aware that I am no taxonomist and deeply conscious of my failings as an angler, I am nevertheless trying to pass along what little I have absorbed of the lore of these masters and to show other sportsmen that there are possibilities they may not have realized in this strenuous game.

Spring of 1935

Spring activities started with a request from Doctor Roy Chapman Andrews, Director of the American Museum, in New York, for a ten-foot specimen of *Isurus dekayi*, the Museum having none. This was a large order for I had never seen a Mackerel Shark as big as that. These sharks follow the schools of mackerel and bluefish to the Jersey Coast in early summer so I set Pete to watching for them.

Pete is a salty two-fisted old Dane who, having for many years wind-jammed around the globe, settled down to running a fish depot at Belmar, New Jersey, and he is my calendar in the local comings and goings of fish. Pete referred me to Steve, a big raw-boned Dalmatian who spends his life among his nets, ten miles or so off the coast. "Ain't seen none this year. Not here yet. Not a damn net torn yet, thank God. I watch. We get 'em. What th'ell yer want uv 'em?" was Steve's monosyllabic reply to my inquiries but he watched faithfully.

If you ever want a common thing, try to find it and learn how rare it is. We watched through May and June. There were Sand Sharks and Duskies and others but not a Mackerel Shark put in his appearance up to the time we sailed for Nassau in June, and Doctor Andrews' order had to go unfilled.

About this time another angler on the Jersey Coast, Mr. Francis Low, caught a White Shark weighing nearly a thousand pounds but he was not promptly allowed a record because the shark is not a game-fish. If, however, that White was like those I have caught, it would be interesting to hear what Mr. Low thinks of his gameness.[1]

1. The American Museum of Natural History, in New York, so appreciated Mr. Low's catch that the fish was mounted and is now an exhibit there.

CHAPTER XIII*

HOW HARD DOES A SHARK PULL?

EXCEPT for a trip or two out on the Jersey Coast and to the Chesapeake, my shark-fishing, in 1934, ended with the Bahamas expedition. I had some flings at the bluefish, a whirl or two at bass on Lake Ontario, some sport with "lakers" and a trip to Canada, with my boys, after trout and salmon. All of this, however, was what a friend calls my genteel fishing and it therefore has no place in these accounts of my association with sharks, my roughneck playmates. That same friend says that my angler ideals have been debased by the notion that a fish to be worth catching must weigh a ton and pull like a switch-engine. That is not true but, incidentally, how hard does a fish pull?

Ask that question in a gathering of anglers and you will stir up a contention in which there will be as many opinions as there are disputants.

I have always believed that the pull of a fish is greatly exaggerated and that he actually does exert a strain on the line which, measured in pounds, would be far less than his own weight. I have even contended that a swimming man might pull harder than a fish of the same weight.

This idea seemed to be disproved when, a year or so ago, in the Princeton University Swimming Pool, with a bass rod and twenty-pound test line, I overcame, in about a quarter of an hour, a member

* The substance of this is reprinted from an article by the author in *Field and Stream*, February, 1936. Courtesy of *Field and Stream*.

[135]

of the Water Polo Team. That stunt proved nothing, however, for being free to move around the pool, I simply nagged the swimmer into exhausting himself, never giving him the chance to use his strength against the tackle.

A MAN ON THE LINE

With the tank available and swimmers willing to cooperate, I now undertook to find out something definite in this question. Mr. H. W. Steppe, the swimming coach, having selected one of his strongest swimmers, we went about the test.

Howard Canoune, the boy chosen, a strapping fellow six feet three inches tall and weighing a hundred and seventy pounds, was thoroughly interested and he was a formidable looking "fish" as we applied the harness to his back.

For this test I used a swordfish rod, a 9/0 reel and No. 30 line and was to remain in place during the struggle. With my swivel chair fast at one end of the pool, I settled in the harness, seated the rod and Canoune plunged in. He swam with a smooth fast crawl while I tightened down the drags until, at about fifty feet away, I had him stopped. Then he changed to a powerful breast stroke and with each surge took out a little line so I had to apply the thumb-pad, but cautiously because tension was very close to the line's breaking point. Between the swimmer's strokes I was able to recover what line he took out with them and his dives and plunges gained him nothing. After fifteen minutes the struggle was practically a stale-mate and, lying back in the harness, my feet braced against the coping, the big rod bowed and the line humming like a tuning fork under its eighty pound strain; I called to Steppe: "I can hold this

[136]

boy but I can't haul him in with this line until he's played out. That's what one does to a fish but there's no sense in doing it here. Of course I can lie back in this chair longer than he can swim." We called Canoune in. He had maintained a pull of from thirty to eighty pounds for nearly twenty minutes which was more than I, at least, had considered possible and he still had perhaps ten minutes left in him.

Throughout the tussle I had been comparing the fight with one against a big fish and, though the man's speed was less and his surges not so violent as those of the fish, his power was amazing. The struggle suggested one with a Tiger Shark, when, in the final stages, he settles down to a slow dogged resistance. And I estimated that Canoune forced me to use as much power as I would have used against a three hundred pound shark.

This naturally suggests the question: "Could that boy exert the pull of a fish of twice his own weight?" My answer is that unquestionably he did. Then how can a shark swim five times as fast as a man could swim? Because the shark's streamline form allows greater speed for less power used and, also, it is to be remembered that the shark is hooked and held by the nose.

The propulsion of a fish is accomplished mainly by his caudal fin, a small though continuously fast-moving propeller whose area pressing against the water may be less than that of the man's arms, hands, legs and feet.

Our next test, a month or so later, was to determine what pull a man could exert on a line held firmly without the spring of the rod. Canoune was harnessed to a stout cod-line at the other end of which was a spring-balance, made fast to a stanchion.

He swam out rapidly with the crawl, coming to the end of the line with a jerk hard enough to send the indicator above fifty pounds. Then, continuing to swim with maximum effort, he held the pull up to between thirty-two to forty pounds.

With the side-stroke, the initial jerk registered a little above fifty pounds, the pull with steady swimming dropping back to from forty to forty-five pounds.

With the breast-stroke the jerk registered eighty pounds and then, with steady swimming, the pull was from eight to eighty— eighty on the strokes, eight on the recoveries.

It would therefore appear that the faster strokes, *crawl* and *side-stroke*, gave a more evenly continuous propulsion and a steadier average tension, but that the slower *breast-stroke*, alternating greater and lighter impulses, more severely tested the line. This may partially explain why the slower man may put a heavier pull on the line than the faster fish.

I can think of many details omitted from these tests, which omissions prevent results from being conclusive comparisons but I will not forestall the pleasure of other anglers in pointing them out.

At least, we had arrived at a rough estimate of the man's pull and, for comparison, it remained for us to harness a fish and to measure his power.

MEASURING THE PULL OF A SHARK

Properly this was to be a hand-line job for the spring of the rod must be eliminated. Neither should there be line-stretch to reduce the pull nor sag and friction to interfere with the movements of the fish. A three-hundred-foot 3/16 inch Manila rope was therefore used and it was passed through the ring of a large spring balance held by two men. Sand Sharks were used for the tests because they are abundant in the Chesapeake Bay at the season when we were making the tests there.

Immediately when a shark was hooked he was drawn rapidly in so he might not exhaust himself by a long fight. Fifty feet from the boat, hauling him ceased and his pull in his surges, when fresh, was measured. Measure was also taken of his average steady pull and then, the men moving backward slowly, we got his resistance when being hauled. The same measures were taken later when the shark was tired and, finally, the shark was brought in close and prodded with a spiked pole to stimulate him to utmost effort.

It is to be borne in mind that different species show quite different characteristics in their fighting. The Mackerel Shark, for example, is both fast and strong. He strikes savagely, surges violently, runs freely and, throughout the struggle maintains a heavy average pull. The Dusky Shark is sluggish but very powerful and maintains a mulish drag which is perhaps even greater than the pull of a Mackerel. The Sand Shark alternates rushes and violent surges with sullen tuggings and, at times, almost ceases to resist. Even in the same species there are great differences in the fighting of individuals, depending largely upon the development and condition of the fish. Males, generally, are more aggressive and enduring than females, and young fully matured adults of large average size, say nine feet long and weighing three hundred pounds, fight harder than either exceptionally large ones or than those less mature. It is therefore necessary to consider with the data obtained in tests also the species and the individuals measured.

In the following tabulation, data are from tests made at the Virginia Capes, August, 1935. The fish were three young, fully matured, male Sand Sharks which, I believe, may be taken as typical. All were in good condition and were fairly hooked in the mouth. Weights were taken when they were dead. Length does not include caudal fin.[1]

Shark	Length Inches	Weight Submgd. Lbs.	Weight Out Lbs.	Pull Surge Fresh Lbs.	Pull Surge Tired	Pull Estim. Reg.
No. 1	108	8	245	99	20	40
No. 2	89	7	176	80	15	30
No. 3	108	9	270	150	20	45
Avg.	102	8	230	110	18	38

From this tabulation it is seen that the typical young male Sand Shark which we were testing was eight feet six inches long. He weighed 230 pounds out of water and 1/28 of that (eight pounds) submerged. When fresh, his pull in surges was 110 pounds, about .48 of a pound for each pound of his weight. His regular pull was only about a third of that and when tired about a sixth.

It is interesting to compare this with the pull of the man on the line which was, in surges, .47 of a pound per pound of weight (about the same as the pull of the shark). In regular pull, however, the man registered about .3 of a pound per pound of weight while the shark registered but .17.

1. Measurements of the pull of abnormal sharks or of those not fairly hooked are not included in this table.

[140]

THE RUN

HE GETS THE IRON

HIS END

Computing these figures to show the pulls of a shark and a man, each weighing 200 pounds, we have:

In surges: man, 94 lbs.; shark, 96 lbs.
Regular: man, 60 lbs.; shark, 34 lbs.

More important, however, from the angler's viewpoint, is comparison of pull of fish with test strengths of lines which is usually three pounds per strand, wet. It will be seen that this 230-pound Sand Shark could have been taken on a No. 39 line, used as hand-line without advantage of spring of rod. Or, with spring of rod and with drags set to slip the line at thirty pounds, he could have been handled on a No. 12.

A 500-pound shark of proportional power would pull in surges, 240 pounds and, regularly, 80 pounds and, tired, 40 pounds. Therefore, with drags set to slip at about 80 pounds, he could be handled on a No. 30 line.

With moving boat, spring of rod to neutralize jerks and a long line to humor rushes, there is no reason why a thousand-pounder could not be taken on a No. 36 and, as a matter of fact, we did, last year in the Bahamas, take a 954-pound Blue Shark on a No. 30 line.

A Sand Shark on Rod

Getting this data was all very interesting and catching the sharks was sport, though hand-line may not be sporty tackle in spite of the fact that the result for the shark is the same as with the rod. Perhaps murder with a club is less commendable than assassination with a rapier. Certainly there is more fun with the rod and, finally, yielding to temptation, I took a holiday from scientific research and started angling.

[141]

The first fish hooked was a nine-foot Sand Shark which went away in a grand rush of three hundred yards against a sixty-pound drag. Then he quit and played "doggo" while I pumped him in to within a hundred feet of the boat and then—away he went again! We had an hour of this seesaw, with occasional soundings, and then he took to running across so that Charlie Bull, the boatman, was busier at fending off the line with a boat-hook than I was with the rod. After a half hour of this, I had the shark up for the iron which Charlie delivered, I think, with delight and vindictiveness.

The excitement on our boat had attracted the attention of other fishermen, several of whom hovered around watching the fight and tooting applause. One of them, a gentleman from New York, came aboard after we had landed our shark to examine the tackle and to learn where to get it. He was completely sold to the sport and I hope he is now having fun at it.

I have digressed to tell of this, because heretofore I have not described a fight with a Sand Shark. Undoubtedly they are not so game as Mackerels and Whites, but, nevertheless, they do often put up an interesting fight. Usually they make several fair rushes alternating with soundings, they are resourceful in making a nuisance of the boat keel and they have a way of waking up when one thinks they are licked.

PULL OF TIGERS

My experiments with the pull of Sand Sharks suggested similar tests with the more powerful Tiger. I therefore got Schuetz, at Nassau, interested and he, being a scientist at heart, made the tests with skill and thoroughness.

Briefly summing up the results, his typical male adult Tiger Shark pulled, in surges, about .53 of a pound for each pound of weight, which is .05 pound greater than that of my Sand Shark, and also his specific gravity was considerably greater.

Like the Sand Shark, however, and like other sharks, the Tiger did not maintain even an approach to his maximum pull for more than very brief periods, but alternated it with relaxations which at times were less than a fourth of it.

It is interesting to consider this in comparison with the wild and almost continuous fury of the swordfish, but also let it be remembered that it is the wild fury of the swordfish which wears him out and that it is this intermittent resting which adds to the difficulty of conquering the shark.

CHAPTER XIV

TO THE BAHAMAS AGAIN

I HAVE never enjoyed more the possession of anything I did not have than "The Bessie," my sixty-foot cruiser, given me by my rich old aunt who never existed but who gave me everything I never received. I have delighted in fishing trips on this boat to seas I never sailed, where I caught fish larger and gamer than ever were.

"The Bessie" is named in honor of this old aunt. She is of ample beam—I mean the boat, of course—heavily Diesel engined and Marconi rigged for emergency. She is reasonably fast, very steady and can withstand any sea. In the after third there are comfortable quarters for four, a tackle room and a little laboratory. Forward there are quarters for the crew and a well-equipped galley. Midship, below the gunwale, is carried the fast twenty-foot fishing boat, ready to be swung outboard.

Our party, including an artist and a zoologist are all keen sportsmen—the crew is tireless and uncomplaining.

Let me advise all fishermen to get a boat like "The Bessie." She costs nothing and in her they can cruise the seven seas—after sharks in the West Indies, after sailfish in Florida, tarpon in the Gulf, tuna at Nova Scotia, broadbills at Catalina, marlins in New Zealand, salmon in Alaska.

When we heard from Schuetz that there were still a few sharks in the Bahamas, "The Bessie" was unfortunately not in commission and we had to seek other transportation.

To the Bahamas Again

One can go from New York to Nassau by the Furness Line, by the Munson Line, or he can go by train to Miami and then ferry or fly across. Our impedimenta precluded flying, ferrying would save little time, the Furness Line had suspended for the season and we were therefore relieved of the necessity of choosing our way.

Hugh and I were again the rodmen, John, with more things to hunt for Doctors Dahlgren and Gudger, was zoologist and parasitologist and, in addition to these multi-syllable titles, he had to take on another, that of photographer, for Coty could not go with us.

Having persuaded Mrs. Wise to go out with us this year, we were to have a second boat on which she could get away from smelly chum and bloody sharks. Profiting by last year's experience, John was to use the second boat for his pickling and photographic activities.

Preparation for an expedition like this is by no means so simple as digging a can of worms and walking to the creek, but in due time, we got our rods, tackle, formalin, cameras and other stuff aboard the "Munargo," at New York, and, June 15, a perfect day, we slipped out through the Narrows and turned south along the familiar New Jersey Coast.

The waters were spotted with fishing craft, one little cruiser passing so close to us that we could see the angler in his swivel chair, harnessed to his tuna rod, his teasers skipping from crest to crest astern. As we passed he got a fine strike and we watched him hull-down still battling the fish.

Porpoises staged their usual entertainments the next day and, following one leaping bounding school of them, I saw the pointed

E. M. SCHUETZ
Resident Manager National Fisheries Corporation, Nassau, N. P.

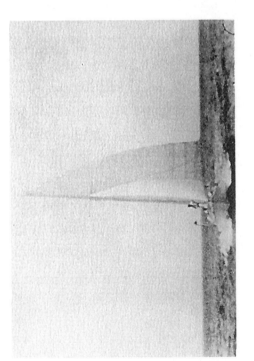

THE MALOLO B.

dorsal and lunate caudal of a Great White Shark—reminding us of our quest, if indeed we needed a reminder.

Tuesday morning we slid into the sun-gilded, palm-fringed harbor of Nassau to be again met by the crowds of chattering natives in wobbly boats, their numbers still undiminished by shark casualties. They howled for coins to be tossed and, there being no code in their business, rugged individualism prevailed, and the best diver got the penny. In the midst of the excitement, a big barracuda slithered along the ship-side. Immediately the swimmers clambered into boats for, fearless of timid sharks, they take no chances with that savage marauder who attacks anything moving in the water.

Schuetz was there to meet us and, after inspection, we confirmed his selection of boats. For the shark-fishing we took the "Malolo B.," the same thirty-nine-foot power boat we had last year, now under command of Captain Burt Bowe, recently promoted, with Bert Hall as crew. For the second boat we took the "Spindrift," a beautiful little thirty-eight-foot Marconi sloop with auxiliary engine—Captain, Willett Sawyer; crew, George Russell. Sitting on the dock coping, it was then and there understood that the two boats were to cruise together and that either or both might be used for shark-fishing, bait-fishing, biology or photography. We would sleep or mess on either boat, wherever and whenever it suited us—we were fishing and would not be interfered with by rules or plans. With those simple articles of agreement our week was absolutely harmonious and even the crew of "The Bessie" could not have been more willing, cheerful and helpfully efficient than were the crews of the "Malolo" and the "Spindrift."

Schuetz was bitten by the sport-bug and accepted the invitation to go with us. For the manager of a shark products corporation and handler of thousands of sharks to go on a fishing trip for pleasure did seem rather like the postman's taking a walk for exercise, but we were delighted to have him.

About the wharves we were objects of no little curiosity to people who wondered at the queer men who had come again to hunt sharks which they did not want when they got them.

In this story of sharking with rod and reel I have tried to limit myself to accounts of sport fishing for sharks, with only a minimum of technical description of species. That would seem to excuse me too from attempting competition with Garman and other real authorities on taxonomy. There is no danger of poaching on Isaac Walton's preserves because he did not go in for shark-fishing and, if they have played the game, modern anglers have kept very quiet about it. Neither is it intended to discuss commercial shark fishing, though popular interest in that comparatively new industry may justify a sketchy account of it, as carried on in the Bahamas.

COMMERCIAL SHARK-FISHING

While few species of sharks may really be classed as game-fish yet, with modern methods of processing and marketing, nearly all of them are of economic value and shark-fishing is carried on extensively all over the world.

In the Bahamas, under the management of Mr. Schuetz, a pioneer in the industry, the sharks are taken in large rope nets. These are about three hundred feet long and fourteen feet deep. Their bottom edges are weighted and anchored and their top edges are held up by cork floats to the net's width above the bottom. Buoys on the surface, fastened by long cords to the net, mark its position.

Having studied the habits of the sharks, seine men stretch the nets across their runways, baiting them with chunks of skate or ray, tied along the lead line. A shark, after the bait, gets a pectoral fin through the net and then, in frantic struggles to free himself, becomes hopelessly entangled. On the next round of the tender tug the net is raised and brawny arms bash what little brains he has from the shark's ugly head with an iron pipe. Then he is hoisted aboard for separation into saleable parts, hide, fins, flesh, oil and teeth. So ends the career of the "Tiger of the Sea"—in shoes or travelling bags, in paint pot or soup bowl, in poultry yard or furrow. All this goes to make up a considerable industry. Last year two thousand sharks were processed in Nassau alone and, conducted with net and club, it may be a profitable business but it is not so with rod and reel for that is sport, and sport is not profitable.

Nassau Again

Wandering about Nassau while the boats were being fuelled and provisioned, it was no different from last year nor, for that matter, from several years ago. "Jessie," whom most visitors know, and other dusky belles, at their wharf-side tables were still prevailing upon tourists to buy gaudy straw hats they did not want and which would be of no use to them at home. Black troubadours, with broken guitars and tuneless songs, cluttered the sidewalks, still singing of their mothers' dislike of peas, rice and cocoanut oil. Houses were as unprepossessing, streets as crowded as ever with nondescript vehicles. If Henry Ford wishes to collect antiquated flivvers, he can find them in Nassau. Or if you want a Victoria "like your grandmother rode in"—there it is. The sun was as hot as last year, the hill was as steep, the old horse was as tired; but the terrace of the Royal Victoria was as shady and the Planter's Punch was as authoritative as ever.

Along the waterfront, children, mere babies, dozens of them, splashed and swam—as much at home in the water as on dry land. They were too young to have learned to swim—they must have been born knowing how. Schuetz says that he never heard of one of them being drowned—but who would know if one were?

CHAPTER XV

BACK TO ANDROS ISLAND

HAVING decided on Andros Island, fifty miles west over open water, our "squadron" sailed at 4:00 P.M. for West End Bay, on New Providence Island, where we would have shelter for the night and be ready to cut across in the morning.

It will be noticed that all through these accounts of vagabonding around the Bahamas, last year and this year, we are repeatedly running for shelter. These waters are none too well charted, coral reefs rise almost to the surface in unexpected places and openings between them are narrow. Black squalls make up with incredible suddenness and burst with fury from sunlit skies. Only a year ago, Captain Sawyer of the "Spindrift" and his two brothers were caught in one of these storms and driven into a creek. When they came out, after being marooned four days they learned that sixteen other boats near them had been wrecked and nineteen men of their crews drowned.

It gets to be annoying to have one's fishing constantly interrupted by the soft voice of the boatman: "Kunnel, it looks pretty bad out yonder—we better run in," but there is reason for it. We had four dirty squalls in six days and any of them might have made trouble for us outside.

We had a good supper on the "Spindrift" where John and Schuetz remained for the night, Mrs. Wise, Hugh and I crossing over to the "Malolo." Her cot was set up in the cockpit while we parked on the transoms.

At daylight we plunged through the reef opening and went bounding along in a smother of spray toward Andros.

This was the sea! The salty fragrant sea! The same in the Bahamas, in Hawaii, off the coast of California, at the Virginia Capes! Why do poets delight in calling this lovely old ocean a monotonous waste when this ever moving surface and these ever changing hues are never the same? Why do they call it desolate when it is so populous and so majestically beautiful? Why do they call it cruel when it gives so generously of its teeming life and provides joy like the present moment? Why does Matthew Arnold call it "The unplummeted, salt, estranging sea"? And even Shakespeare, when he wants to say the worst about his most diabolical character, calls Iago a "Spartan dog, more fell than anguish, hunger, or *the sea!*"

All this imponderable mass of water, surging in waves, flying in spray, or, in sheltered places, as pellucid as the air itself, is full of life—life down from giant whales to specks not large enough to deflect light rays, but all these atoms of life are being transformed by nature's process into viscous jellyfish, into firm flesh and into even hard coral rock. Can we look at this mill of God, in operation, and call it desolate; can we see it manufacture food for us and call it cruel; can we see its varied activities and call it monotonous?

GREEN CAY, BLACK TIPS, SQUALLS

We trolled on the way across for barracuda and arrived at Green Cay with chum and bait enough to start shark-fishing, but Mrs. Wise and John went off in the "Spindrift" to catch Spanish mackerel for our mess and to lay in an extra supply of bait.

I took the chair, Hugh standing by and Schuetz in reserve, and promptly I hooked a shark which sand-papered my line and got away. To the skillful angler the breaking of tackle is rather of a discredit, but there may be excuse for it when fighting sharks, for their great weight and their ability to bite or to cut the line, may part it in spite of the angler's skill. A swordfisher once said to me: "I never break tackle—I use skill—I am above using brute strength." "Oh, yeah?" I replied. That fellow was like the man who never hung his fly in the alders—just a liar.

After repairs to the tackle I remained in the chair for another shark and that fellow was a lively one—he applied his force along the three usual coordinates and also used Einstein's time dimension. Making his circles, he varied depth so his course was like the track of a rollercoaster. "Look at him!" I yelled in admiration—"Round and round—Oh-h-h—but he comes out here"—and he did, to get the iron and to die as that crazy song will die.

Hugh now relieved me and brought two more sharks to iron, Black Tips, not big but very game. He was relieved by Schuetz whose first experience this was with heavy fish on tackle and in spite of our coaching, or maybe because of it, he lost two sharks and some line.

Sharks were coming fast and the "Spindrift" was keeping us well supplied with bait but, now Nemesis came in the form of Burt with his "Kunnel, dey's a squall comin'," so we ran for shelter behind the reef where the "Spindrift" came foaming in to join us.

I wish I were poet enough to describe a tropical squall amongst these islet gems. Nobody could do that; but I would try it—just for my own pleasure—just to watch that black speck in the sky come closer, closer, and grow larger, larger; to hear the breeze, now murmuring in the palms, swell to a deafening roar; to see the surf, now rolling gently against the reef, surge up and smash over it in mountainous combers whose crests are bases of flying walls of feathery spray. All the rich colors on land change, through pastel tints, to subtle shades of grey; the emerald and sapphire sea becomes leaden-hued flecked with white. Palms, which stood so regally erect, bow like reeds before the blast, and fronds torn from them scud like birds before the gale. Could anything be more superb! But it does upset our fishing.

So far, the sharks we had caught were Black Tips—game little fellows, but disappointing in size because this species is usually not much over a hundred pounds in weight. To my eyes, they were patriotically clothed in grey with black trimmings and they were as lithe as the West Point cadets whose colors they wore. During the rest of the day we continued to get only Black Tips, none weighing more than two hundred pounds, and with our heavy tackle we horsed them in with little ceremony.

At first this puzzled me because last year at this same place we got only big Tigers. Finally, however, I hit upon an explanation. Around the island the bottom slopes away gradually at first and then drops off sharply to great depth. Last year, with an offshore wind, we had anchored out as far as our cable could reach bottom and from there floated our bait out into the deep water where big sharks were. This year, the strong on-shore wind had prevented our doing this and we were picking up the little sharks in shallow water. This, like other theories, is simply an hypothesis to explain a known fact, the fact being that we got no large sharks where we did get them last year.

Some sharks, especially Duskies, will not run, but prefer to simply lie back and tug—Black Tips are inclined to be like that. To

THE LITHE GREY FORM UNDER THE SURFACE

BURT GIVES HIM THE IRON

wear out such a fish, the rodman must wear himself out pumping. To handle a mule like that, we developed a special treatment and called it "taking him for a ride." The boat was kicked along slowly while the rodman lay back in his harness, watching strain on his line and slipping line when necessary, while the engine did the "pumping." It is worth mentioning that such a "ride" seemed to be particularly distasteful to most sharks and that often in the midst of it, they woke up and went to fighting.

Burt showed during this first day the effects of last year's training. At the call of "Strike" the gong, now a little oil drum, went over and he had his boat always where the rodman wanted it. Under John's direction, Captain Sawyer learned to have the "Spindrift" in place for photography, and between fights to have Mrs. Wise on the barracuda grounds. Sharks were plentiful, our organization was about perfect, but the fly in the ointment was the size of the sharks. In fishing there's always some damned thing that isn't right!

Fresh Creek, More Sharks and More Squalls

The weather that night drove us behind the reef off Fresh Creek. There we put over the "Bottom-light," a contrivance I had made of a sixty-four candle power bulb in a sealed Mason jar. It illuminated the bottom like day five fathoms down and enabled us to see a number of fish, attracted by the light, including a shark, but neither on that night nor on succeeding ones were we able to anchor out beyond the reef where we might have seen more. I had hoped to tether a wounded shark down there and to observe how his comrades treated him.

In daytime one never tires of watching what goes on at the bottom. Over the boatside, through the water glass, one looks five fathoms down through the crystal water, at herds of multi-colored fish browsing over marine vegetation among coral boulders, like cattle on the green pastures of the dry land.

These littoral grazing fields, here and there broken by stretches of bare sand, slope undulating gently away toward a shelf where they are to plunge precipitously to abysmal depths at the ocean floor; where no ray of light penetrates, to illuminate a desert of mud strewn with debris and waste from above:

> . . . deep as the ooze and bottom of the sea
> With sunken wreck and sunless treasuries.

But even down at those depths, in that inky darkness, there is life for creatures which can withstand the terrific pressure, creatures which carry their own lights in the form of phosphorescence, or which substitute a marvelous tactile sense for sight. Oozy, slimy, infinitesimal things cling to the mud and the giant squid, never voluntarily coming to the upper levels, cruises in the half light between them and the bottom. All the way down, struggle for existence goes on—minute creatures prey upon one another and the sperm whale devours the giant squid.

Just beneath the boat, on the upper floor of this green and gold palace, we see the struggle in progress. A mollusk-eating fish crushes a mussel from its shell as on land a robin might draw a worm from its hole; but as a hawk might swoop upon the robin, a barracuda darts at the fish to be attacked in turn by a shark.

> Big bugs have little bugs
> And those bugs have lesser bugs
> To get on their backs and bite 'em
> And so ad infinitum.

[156]

Here, as on land, life spreads death to maintain itself, but even creatures which we smugly call "predatory" kill only to provide themselves with food. These very sharks, slashed and bleeding, trailing at the boatside, however, were killed for sport alone and, though man may try to justify himself by saying he saved the lives of many other fish by killing the sharks; did nature assign him to be their executioner?—"Wha-a-a!" goes the reel and meditation ends with another shark fight.

The forenoon of Thursday we brought to iron several Black Tips and then, the weather having turned more favorable, we moved out over the ledge and got our baits into deep water where Hugh took a fair-sized Brown. Then another squall drove us in behind the reef at Green Cay.

Nine sharks in two days! Good sport and a lot of back-breaking exercise! A catch of fifteen hundred pounds would be unheard of on a trout brook or even on a salmon stream, but to us big-game hunters these sharks, not one of them above three hundred pounds, were minnows and my temper was becoming a little ragged. I had set my heart on a thousand pound Tiger, and was probably discounting the really grand sport we were having with smaller sharks that were full of fight.

I would hate to say that a big shark does not fight as hard as one not so large, but certain it is that a four- or five-hundred-pounder has often seemed to give me more battle per pound. But we were not catching five-hundred-pounders and I was getting fed up with Black Tips inside the reefs. Burt's prudence was reasonable but after all, thought I, we are not hiring him as guardian and I told him testily: "Get out over that reef, if you lose your damned boat!" Burt looked at me mournfully and obeyed, but outside I was proved wrong as well as bad tempered, for wind and tide did not allow us to get our hooks down where I thought the big Tigers would be.

Then we went out further and fished drifting in, but the wind carried us along so fast that we were in effect trolling over the irregular bottom, sometimes fishing too shallow and sometimes snagging the coral boulders, so we had no success at that. I had lashed myself into a fury, though I had no Tiger tail to do it with, and my humor was not improved by seeing three beautiful marlin swordfish go leaping past when we were not equipped to follow them.

A nasty squall that evening drove Mrs. Wise below into the cabin of the "Spindrift," the two boys going with her while Schuetz and I held down the cockpit of the "Malolo." The squall came on with an ugly half hour of howling wind which ripped loose the deck curtains and drenched us with sheets of water. The tossing boats strained at their cables but anchors held and thankful we were to be behind the reef where thundering rollers broke into lines of white foam. It would really be most unpleasant to be wrecked at night when you could not see where you were being drowned. As suddenly as it had begun, the squall ceased. Now, on the reef there was but the rhythmic pound of subsiding seas, and we lay snug upon a glassy moonlit little bay, where from the nearby island shore silvery palms pointed to gleaming tropical constellations. The storm was over and with it had cleared up my disappointment and bad humor. Stretched out on the transoms we dropped off to sleep—to dream of tomorrow.

At sunup both boats went out again; Hugh, Schuetz and I after sharks, on the "Malolo"; Mrs. Wise and John, after barracudas, on the "Spindrift."

Mrs. Wise had become our dependence for bait. If she had ever before this trip caught fish anywhere except on a dinner-plate, I never knew of it but she was now expert and handled her barracudas with deadly efficiency. For us sharks had been running small but barracudas were averaging twenty pounds and she got one close to thirty. Besides the hundred pounds or more of bait and chum, the "Spindrift" had to supply us each day with fish for our mess of nine people, and it provided Spanish mackerel, snappers and the like. It supplied even more than we could eat so the surplus went for chum. Thus to throw away fine edible fish is not so wasteful and sinful as it might seem because nature intends them to be food for other creatures who eat every particle of them. A crab eats a dead fish and another fish eats the crab, to be eaten in turn by a shark. What a slaughter pen this world is—wet or dry!

Even after the rodmen had hung their rods in the racks and Mrs. Wise had wound up her line, the biologist was still busy; for each day, having photographed the fights, dissected the carcasses and pickled specimens, there were mollusks, corals and seaweeds with queer shapes and Latin names, to be hunted for on the shoals.

If anything was needed to convince our Carib boatmen of the queerness of our party, John's activities supplied it, and one of the crew was heard to remark: "Two of 'em fishin' for things so big yer couldn't lift 'em on a derrick—one huntin' for things so small yer can't see 'em—the lady catchin' poison fish."

In spite of the difficulty of John's photographic work he got a lot of fine pictures. We were less successful with the single shot camera because there was rarely time to change to it. Even with the movie camera it is not easy to get pictures of a shark fight because the fish has a way of staging his struggle where it suits him rather than where the cameraman would like it. The rodman is too absorbed in his job to pose for the photographer, even if he could, and the cameraman, behind the rodman, where he has to be if he is in the boat with him, will probably get a foreshortened picture of a minnow on a long tapering rope tied to a telegraph pole in the hands of a giant. If in another boat, the cameraman will probably have the fishing boat between him and the shark. After the fight is over there is likely to be a conversation like this: "Did you get that grand surge when he rushed toward the boat?" "No, I could see nothing in the finder but your helmet." "Did you get him when he was skittering on the surface?" "No, your boat was in the way."—! ! !

CHAPTER XVI

THE LAST OF THE SHARKS
UNWILLINGLY HOME

SCHUETZ was in the chair Friday morning when a saucy little six-foot shark, after nosing the ball around for a while, bit off the line above it, and bait, hook and leader, still floated by the ball, drifted away. When recovered by the dory they were put back on the line and Schuetz casting out again, caught the offender and brought him to iron. It was characteristic of the savagery of sharks that this one, with the hook in his mouth and the dart in his side attacked the bait barracudas trailing at the gunwale and had one of them tight in his teeth when Burt used the lance.

This suggests my recurring to the vitality of sharks and again speaking of my method of ending a fight. I realize that my way of landing a big shark may be criticized as not entirely in accord with the usual ethics of deep-sea angling. Like others, I prefer the gaff-hook for tuna but, like any sportsman, I wish to see my swordfish hauled over the gunwale by his bill. For obvious reasons, however, it is not wholesome to seize a shark by the nose and a gaff-hook would be wrenched from the hands of the boatman. Sharks do not arrive at the boatside exhausted but often with enough power and fight left to make the use of the gaff impossible. Right or wrong, therefore, I have arrived at the conclusion that when the leader comes in, the rodman's fight is won and that it may be properly ended with the dart and lance and, incidentally, it is not easy to drive the dart through the denticled hide of a shark.

TIGERS OF THE SEA

I have described but a few of my fights with sharks. Each struggle differs from another somewhat but all are more or less alike. It is excitement that holds the angler, in spite of aching back, limp shoulders and numb arms. The reader who does not hear the reel shriek, who does not feel the rod bend, who does not see the monster shark churn and splash, cannot be expected to share this excitement. He knows not the breath-taking suspense when his line will bear no more strain, nor the exhilaration when the iron strikes home.

NORTH BIGHT—HAMMERHEADS

Before sunset we chugged into North Bight and anchored in two fathoms of water over a flat sand bottom strewn with mollusks. We did not expect to find sharks there except, possibly, a Nurse Shark and we were not hunting for them. We were all fed up with Black Tips outside and we did want a good supper and a long sleep where the boats might, for a while, cease their everlasting plunging.

While the "Malolo" was making fast to the "Spindrift" and just as Sawyer was about to call, "come and get it," a twelve-foot Hammerhead, gliding on the surface, circled the boats. Hugh jumped to the chair and floated out a bait as fast as the slow tide would carry it. Another Hammerhead slithered in and the two began playing with the float ball, ignoring the bait, a foot or two below it. The ball, monopolizing too much of the sharks' attention, was removed and the bait was carried out by the dory and thrown over. Soon the sharks were circling it, their high fins making white rings on the surface, while all hands in the boats, forgetting supper, watched and held their breath. After a half hour of Hammerhead hesitation, one of them swirled down at the bait—took it!—and

[162]

dashed off in a smother of foam, the reel singing high tenor. Hugh gave him time and then, rising in his chair, struck hard. All drags set, he lay back in the harness and the fish went into a beautiful run with no indication that he would ever stop, while I, having seen the size of the shark, shouted: "Happy days are here again!" Then the Hammerhead, true to type, reversed his tiller and came charging toward the boat faster than Hugh could wind. As he passed, Hugh threw the free-spindle lever, pressed the thumb-pad, and gingerly screwed down drags, but, with a great splash, the shark breached the surface—the bait flew into the air—he was gone! He had never had the hook—all that pull was made while holding the bait in his teeth and he had bitten it in half—a Hammerhead trick!

But these sharks were not yet through with their irritating tricks and now they came to within fifty feet of the boat and there, in plain view, settled placidly to the bottom. No amount of tempting, not even the dragging of the bait over their noses, induced either of them to take it again, and finally they swam leisurely away.

I think I have told before how cautious and tricky a Hammerhead can be. Here is another instance of it—they are almost intelligent!

No Luck

Both boats were outside early Saturday morning, trolling for bait, for we had chummed away all we had, after those Hammerheads. Nevertheless, we got to shark-fishing promptly because we were able to buy some large parrotfish from a native fisherman and he agreed, too, to get us some skates or rays.

After swinging with the heavy roll for three hours in the swivel

TIGERS OF THE SEA

chair, back and forth, back and forth, the hot sun pounding through my helmet and the heavy rod jerking at the harness, I called for relief and stepped down. Burt, holding the rod during the change, remarked facetiously: "Sharks surely are plentiful! In thirty seconds I'll have one!" Then he began counting: "One—Two—Three—Four—" The rod was jerked nearly out of his hands and Hugh, jumping to the chair, grabbed it from him. The drags were, of course, eased for the transfer, and, before Hugh could tighten them, the fish, heading straight down, cut the line on the coral at the bottom.

An hour later, Hugh had another and a heavy strike, the fish going out in a nice rush and then sounding. The stubbornness with which he fought convinced us that at last we had a little Tiger Shark, but, a half hour later, Hugh hauled in an immense grouper—disappointment, but a lot of chum, and we needed it.

The remainder of the day, inside, outside, and over the reef, we fished conscientiously, chummed heavily, and baited lavishly, but we got no strike from a shark. They simply were not there, and so ended the first day on which I was ever "skunked" in the Bahamas.

We might have been justified in being bad humored that evening, but we were not at all grouchy, for fishing had been so poor that it was funny and we had to laugh.

We anchored again for the night in North Bight, and at sunset the native from whom we had engaged the rays brought us one of about a hundred pounds. His little boat, hull, sails and rigging, were all made by himself, as was also his crew, which consisted of three small sons varying in size from that of a barracuda to that of a Black Tip. "Lower the main sheet!" he commanded in nautical style, as he ran alongside. "Down, suh!" replied the smallest and blackest of the crew, as the flour-sack peak dropped. Then the middle-sized boy began sculling the craft to our gunwale.

WEST END BAY

Certainly we had been licked at North Bight and, since the weather looked bad in the morning, we ran for West End Bay to be in easier reach of Nassau.

We had our ray for chum and on the way across we picked up a number of barracudas and other fish for bait, so we went to shark-fishing immediately on arrival at West End Bay. Soon we took a Sand Shark which put up a slow logy fight, and then Schuetz, in the chair, got a real strike. Against all drags, his line sizzled out and he was almost lifted from his seat. Then, a stubborn sounding, another rush, and more sounding. Schuetz had taken his regular turns in the chair during the week and he was no longer a tyro at the game. His fingers now went automatically to the proper drags and levers and he handled his rod and pumped like a veteran.

After an hour we got a glimpse of the lithe brown form of a ten-foot Tiger Shark. How graceful he was as he swirled and lunged and looped and rolled! Five hundred pounds of fighting devil! Again and again, after line-scorching rushes, down he went for persistent tugs when the hook might as well have been fast in the coral. Each plunge of the boat took out feet or fathoms of line to be laboriously pumped back. "What are you doing to that fish?" I asked, but Schuetz, unable to speak, simply looked his reply: "What is he doing to me?" I knew just how Schuetz felt. It was one of those times when, if the angler could compromise with the fish, he would be sorely tempted to do so.

[165]

An hour later, the Tiger was showing signs of weakening and there was probably not much more than an hour of fight left in him. His rushes were shorter and he was being held close in for longer periods. Schuetz was winning his fight! At this moment the shark was but fifty feet from the boat and was being temporarily held there when—a flash of grey shot under our stern. A huge Dusky dashed upon the tethered Tiger and tore from his side a great chunk of flesh. Over and over, together rolled the two sharks, swirling toward the bottom, and, under the added strain the line—parted!

Other sharks attracted as sharks always are by the struggles of one in trouble were around us and they would now follow the wounded shark away. To hold them close by, until the tackle could be repaired, I ordered overboard the rope emergency line lying on the deck baited with a large chunk of ray. The Dusky had abandoned his attack when the Tiger got free and he promptly seized the bait. Burt threw a turn around a cleat and slowly paid out rope while the seven hundred pounds of fury surged, looped and leaped. The hook was too solidly set to tear out, the rope was too strong to break and four men heaved the Dusky to the boatside to be executed by Burt with the lance—the villain who had spoiled a grand game for Schuetz!

Observe now, that this Dusky attacked when the Tiger was held on Schuetz' line and could not defend himself, but that he abandoned his attack as soon as the line broke. I did not fail to point out all this to Schuetz with whom I had constantly disagreed about the courage of sharks, he contending that it is not cowardice but judgment which makes them cautious. At any rate a shark's conduct, cowardice or judgment, is in marked contrast with the unreasoning gallantry of a gamecock which enters a fight regardless of odds.

RUNNING OFF ENERGY   A BIG DUSKY

WILL HE EVER STOP?

Courage must not, however, be too much tempered with judgment or, if it were, many of us soldiers who are wearing decorations for gallantry would not have them. But what is that to a shark?

That night we anchored in West End Bay and Monday, our last day, we were fishing early but, in spite of conscientious work, we got no sharks. Before we left anchorage, however, the zoologist spied two beautiful striped sucker fish hanging around the dead shark which was tied to the dory. He rigged up a pack-thread line with pin-hook, baited it with raw potato, and caught one of them. The other would not bite. Perhaps he was holding back for Mayonnaise on his salad.

The "Munargo" was sailing from Nassau at five o'clock and we had to be there—we had to surrender all of this private proprietorship of the sea and become part of a herd of passengers on a liner! We were going to change broad waters for narrow corridors; blue waves lapping at the gunwale for sport-clad people lounging at the rail; the song of the reel for jazz music; salt spray for cigarette smoke and perfumery—and then the city, Ugh!

At eleven o'clock Mrs. Wise, John and Schuetz, in the "Spindrift," sails bulging and mast bending, went plunging off but Hugh and I, in the "Malolo" watched them hull down while we stayed for yet another shark. We just could not bear to quit and Hugh, last in the chair, did not wind in until our anchor was up. "Hugh," I said, "we've got to stop and, anyway, you know this is not worth while for it is not *sport angling*—the shark is not a game-fish." Looking at his blistered hands, Hugh replied: "Who says so?"

One might think that six days in a little tossing boat, through four squalls, ought to have taken the edge off our keenness but they had not, and, while we packed the rods we were planning to have them out again on the Jersey Coast.

[167]

"There are queer things in this old ocean," I was thinking as I settled into a comfortable chair with a pillow, not a harness, on my back. "There are fishes that swallow fishes and those which puff up so they cannot be swallowed. Some kill their game with electric shocks and one is equipped with rod, line and dangling lure. Some grunt and some whistle. Many are blind but one wears bifocal spectacles for looking above and below.

"Man has told some weird tales about Mermaids and Shipholders but his imagination is put to shame by the real inventions of Nature. Hugh and I think we have taken large sharks but how about the great Whale Sharks which cruise this very sea—Old Zapadilla Tom, seventy feet long and weighing tons"—Bump!—That's not he—It's the "Munargo" and our shark hunt is over.

Sunburned skins and sore muscles attest, as we climb the ladder, that we have had a glorious week. We did not get the "thousand-pounder" but we did get a lot of them which were not minnows and the thousand-pounder will be excuse for our next trip. We'll get him yet!—"*On les aura!*"

On the voyage home, a fellow passenger returning from a fishing trip to Nassau, athrill and trying to thrill others in the smoking room with his experiences with barracudas, asked me if I was acquainted with that big savage fish. "Yes," I replied, "we use them for bait."

In the Gulf Stream, the high "gaff-topsail" of a Hammerhead followed in our wake and I found myself longing to have him on my line—"WHY?" That is a question which friends have been asking me for years. A question they would be asking when I arrived home. A question which, still, I cannot answer.

Why should a man go to considerable expense and live for a

week on a tossing little boat, with few comforts and lots of hard work, for the sole purpose of matching his wits and strength against those of a fish, when he does not want the fish anyway?

I can explain this no more than Carl Akeley could have explained the fascination of the African jungle—no more than Admiral Byrd can explain the delights of an Arctic igloo.

Perhaps it is the primitive instinct some of us have inherited from cave-man ancestors and which centuries of civilization have not eradicated but, thank God, love of the chase is still in me, so

WIND IN!

APPENDIX I

SOME SHARK SPECIES—PARTICULARLY OF THE NORTH ATLANTIC

INCLUDED with the hope that this appendix may assist anglers in identifying their catch. Some unusual species are included as of possible general interest. For more complete information, the reader is referred to the following named authorities from which data for this book were freely taken.

Bigelow and Schroeder, *Canadian Atlantic Fauna Elasmobranchii*, Univ. of Toronto Press, 1934.

Bigelow and Schroeder, *Notes on North West Atlantic Sharks*, Bull. Mus. Comp. Zool., Vol. 68, 1927.

Bigelow and Welsh, *The Fishes of the Gulf of Maine*, U. S. Bureau of Fisheries, 1925.

Breder, C. M., Jr., *Papers and Bulletins*, N. Y. Aquarium, Brooklyn Museum, and *Science Magazine*, 1920–1936.

California State Fish and Game Commission, *California Fish and Game*, Vol. 3, No. 4, 1917.

Daniel, J. F., *The Elasmobranch Fishes*, Third Edition, University of California Press, 1934.

Frey, Heinrich Herman, *Icthyobiblia*, "Jonah and the Great Fish," pp. 30–49, Leipzig, 1594.

Garman, Samuel, *The Plagiostomia*, Museum of Comparative Zoology, Harvard University, 1913.

Gregory and LaMonte, *The World of Fishes*, Am. Mus. Natl. History, 1934.

Gudger, E. W., *Cannibalism among Sharks and Rays, Poison Fishes, The Whale Shark* and other papers, Am. Mus. Natl. History.

Jordan and Everman, *Fish of North and Middle America*, Smithsonian Institution, 1896.

Linnaeus, Carl von, *Septuna Naturae*, Tenth Edition (the *Standard*), 2 Vols., Stockholm, 1758–59. (This Tenth Edition is the international date line for scientific names of animals.)

New York Zoological Society, *Bulletins*, 1931.

Nichols and Breder, *Marine Fishes of New York and Southern New England*, New York Zoological Society, 1927.

Nichols and Murphy, *Long Island Fauna IV, The Selachil*, Brooklyn Museum, 1916.

Roule, Louis, *Fishes, Their Journeys and Migrations*, W. W. Norton, N. Y., 1933.

Smithsonian Institution, U. S. Natnl. Museum, *Bulletin 47*, 1900.

U. S. Geographic Society, *Book of Fishes*, U. S. Geographic Society, Washington, D. C., 1924.

Young and Mazet, *Shark! Shark!*, Gotham House, N. Y., 1934.

THE GREAT WHITE SHARK
(*Carcharodon carcharias*)

THE Great White Shark is one of the largest, most powerful and most ferocious of our North Atlantic species. He is to be considered as the true *man-eater* for against him the charge of anthropophagy is conclusively sustained.

In length this species is said to attain a maximum of forty feet but it is rarely taken of more than half that length. He is found in both temperate and tropical seas and, though essentially a rover of the broad ocean, he, being a live-fish-feeder, often follows schools into coastal waters.

His fusiform body, massive forward, terminates in a rather slender tail, or peduncle, on which there are characteristic lateral keels and caudal pits.

The conical head, slightly wider than deep at the nostrils, terminates in a rather blunted snout and it is a little more than a fourth the total length of the fish. Eyes, with erect pupils, are over the front edge of the large crescent-shaped mouth.

Teeth are large, triangular and serrate, twenty-six in the upper jaw row, twenty-four in the lower. Teeth of the upper row are the broader and the third teeth on each side of the middle of this row are smaller than those adjacent to them.

Gill-openings are wide and the spaces between first and second openings are about four times as great as spaces between the fourth and fifth.

The curved front edges of the large pectorals are nearly twice as long as the bases and the back edges are almost straight. First dorsal is moderate in size, triangular in shape and is slightly longer than high. Its top is rather pointed and the entire fin is forward of the middle of the fish. Second dorsal, small, is forward of anal. Ventrals are moderate. Caudal, large and lunate, upper lobe the longer.

The back of this fish is pale slaty-brown, shading to white on sides and belly. There are dark spots on pectorals. Ventrals, white elsewhere, are olive on front edges.

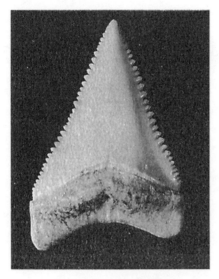

WHITE SHARK
Carcharodon
Broadly triangular, coarsely serrate

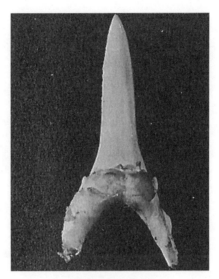

PORBEAGLE
Lamna nasus
Long, curved, narrow and pointed. Cusps on both sides of base

MACKEREL SHARK
Isurus tigris
Long, curved, pointed, narrow. Without cusps

NEW ZEALAND MAKO
Isuropsis mako
Similar to teeth of *I. tigris*. No cusps

Courtesy of American Museum of Natural History

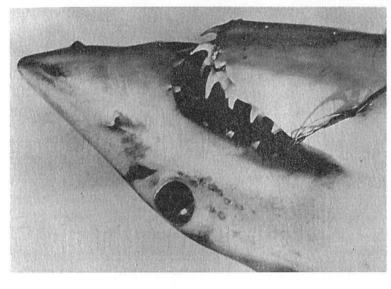

HEAD OF THE
NEW ZEALAND MAKO
Caught by Zane Grey
Notice the sharp snout, glittering black
eyes and teeth and you will see that we
do not catch this fish in our waters

THE NEW ZEALAND MAKO
Isuropis mako
Caught by Zane Grey, the Dean of the
Mako anglers

APPENDIX I

The characteristic coloring of this shark, the dark pectoral spots, the olive-edged ventrals, the robust body with tapering keeled peduncle and especially his teeth make identification easy.

THE MACKEREL SHARKS
(*Carcharodon, Isurus, Lamna*)

STRICTLY speaking, the Mackerel Shark is *Isurus tigris*, synonym *Isurus dekayi*, but the name is used for all members of the family in which there are three distinct genera: *Isurus*, Mackerel Shark; *Lamna*, Porbeagle Shark, and *Carcharodon*, White Shark or Man-Eater.

This family is of especial interest to the sportsman because in it are found most of the sharks which will take the bait trolling and also most of the gamest sharks.

We may omit here discussion of the *Carcharodon*, which has already been considered, under the name of Great White Shark, and think now, in our waters, of only the Mackerel Shark (*Isurus*) and the Porbeagle (*Lamna*), and, in the South Seas, the Mako which the ichthyologist of the Australian Museum classifies as a distinct species, *Isuropsis Mako* (Whitley).

These species all have the characteristic long-pointed snout and are otherwise so similar that the most definite distinction between them is the teeth. In both Mackerel Shark and Porbeagle, teeth are pointed, narrow, long, and slightly curved, but on both sides of the bases of the teeth of the Porbeagle there are small cusps while there are no cusps on the teeth of the Mackerel Shark. This distinction, however, becomes difficult in the case of the Mako (I mean the New Zealand Mako) for, as with the Mackerel Shark, his teeth have no cusps. One of the most readily recognized differences seems to be that the eyes of the Mako are black and glittering instead of amber, as with most sharks.

Lately there has been a lot of talk about "Makos" caught on our Atlantic coast. Obviously, the name has been used to include all genera of the Mackerel Shark family, *Isurus, Lamna,* and *Carcharodon*. It is a natural mistake for fishermen and anglers unfamiliar with distinctions between these sharks. Few of them have seen a Mako, and pictures which they may have seen can hardly show the differences. The confusion will probably continue until fishermen learn these differences—that will be never. In the meantime, anglers wish to catch Makos, and guides, striving to please, provide them.

"Mako" is a name of Maori origin, bearing no relation to "Mackerel." The fish

(*Isuropsis mako*) is similar to our Mackerel Shark, and is at least cousin to him, but he attains greater size and he frequently leaps, which our sharks rarely do. He belongs to the South Seas, and I very much doubt that he ever comes to our waters.

I go into all this because, sooner or later, your guide will probably tell you that you have caught a Mako. I hope he will be right, but more likely you will have caught a Mackerel Shark or a Porbeagle. I have never seen a Mako in our Atlantic, and I do not believe there are any there. I am willing to change this opinion, but I have to be shown.

A number of times, in the past two years, I have been shown "Makos" on the New Jersey coast and in Nova Scotia. In every case but one, however, the fish, on examination, proved to be a Porbeagle and the exception was a Mackerel Shark.

Differentiating between the Mackerel Shark (*I. tigris*) and the Porbeagle (*L. nasus* and *L. cornubica*) one should notice his higher, sharper first dorsal, his narrower, longer pectorals, his narrower caudal, and his sharper snout. Bigelow and Schroeder (in *Chordata 12*) call the Porbeagle the Common Mackerel Shark, and the *I. tigris* the Sharp Nose Mackerel Shark.

Zane Grey, who undoubtedly has had more experience with the Mako than has any other American angler, calls him the "Aristocrat of Sharks," "New Zealand's Premier Sporting Fish."

In articles written by him for *Natural History Magazine,* January, 1928, and May, 1934, Dr. Grey recounts the excitement of fighting these monsters which weighed in the neighborhood of a quarter of a ton and leaped like trout.

Since we cannot expect to get Makos in our waters, we may as well consider the nearest sharks we have to them—their cousins, the Mackerel Shark and the Porbeagle. These fierce pelagic fish-feeders attain a length of at least ten feet and are found on the Atlantic coast from the Gulf of Mexico to Nova Scotia, the Porbeagle also is found on the Pacific coast. Their struggles on the line may quite equal those of the tuna and, at times, may be comparable with those of the swordfish.

In both species, the fusiform body is moderately robust, the peduncle tapering but not slender. From tip to tip, the outline of the fish is made up of two sweeping curves, with no sudden change of direction, and there is no conspicuous belly. The very build of these fishes is indicative of the power and speed they possess.

It is important to notice, too, the keel-like ridges along both sides of the peduncle and the pits or depressions on its top and bottom.

The head, about a fourth of the total length of the fish, is conical and terminates in a long sharp snout.

[174]

APPENDIX I

The mouth is large, but narrow-crescent shaped.

In the Mackerel Shark (*I. tigris*), teeth are sharp-pointed, narrow, long, slightly curved, and finely serrate. Those of the upper jaw are more curved than those of the lower jaw which are almost straight. Teeth are in 26/26 rows.

The teeth of the Porbeagle are similar to those of the *I. tigris*, but there are cusps at the bases and the teeth are in 26/24 rows.

Pectorals are long, curved, and pointed; their length about twice their base. First dorsal, a little behind pectorals, is moderate in size and slightly wider than high. Second dorsal is small and a little forward of the anal. Ventrals are about midway between pectorals and caudal. Caudal is large and lunate, its tips very sharp, and the upper lobe is one-fourth longer than the lower.

The color of these sharks is bluish-grey to ashy-brown, shading to white beneath, the color changing sharply at the level of the caudal keels.

The *Isurus* has narrower, longer pectorals, narrower dorsal and caudal, higher and sharper first dorsal, and sharper snout than the *Lamna cornubica* shown on a preceding page, to which it is otherwise similar.

Mr. J. T. Nichols, Curator of Modern Fishes, American Museum of Natural History, who should certainly be considered an authority, believes that there is but one *Isurus* on our eastern coast (*Isurus tigris* or *dekayi*). Miss LaMonte, Associate Curator, informs me that there is no *Isurus* recognized on our western coast, the Bonito Shark there being the *Lamna nasus*.

THE TIGER SHARK
(*Galeocerdo tigrinus*)

THIS large and savage species properly belongs in tropical and subtropical waters and is abundant in the Bahamas and the West Indies where it is so feared that the mention of Tiger Shark sends cold chills through the natives. He is common, too, in the Gulf of Mexico and off the coast of Florida and, while not so usual, he is found further north, to Cape Lookout.

His average length is perhaps ten or twelve feet though he frequently attains fifteen and has been alleged to reach thirty feet.

His body, though elongate, is massive and his head, wider than high at the snout, is broad and short. The snout is almost semicircular in outline and the mouth is very large.

Teeth, conspicuously large, are alike in both jaws, twenty-one in upper front row, twenty-five in lower. They are broad sickle-shaped and serrate, with edges character-istically notched.

Pectorals, not quite falciform, are large and curved, length a little less than twice the base, points rounded. First dorsal, moderate in size, triangular, somewhat longer than high, is placed back of pectorals. The small second dorsal starts a little forward of the anal and its distance from the caudal is twice its own length. Caudal is lunate, long, slender and pointed, the upper lobe being much the longer.

The young of this species are brownish-grey on the back and white on the belly. On back and sides there are small dark rings, the inside of which is greyish-white. As the young develop these rings fuse and disappear and the white inside of them, also fusing, appears as irregular stripes which become faint as the shark matures, though on some fully grown sharks they are still discernible between the second dorsal and caudal. It is these spots and bands which naturally suggest the common names—*Tiger Shark, Leopard Shark, Spotted Shark*. In old fish the color becomes a more or less uniform greyish-brown.

THE GREAT BLUE SHARK
(*Galeus glaucus—Prionace glauca*)

THIS is another big pelagic species and another shark charged with being a man-eater. Primarily he belongs in warm waters but he is found all along our Atlantic coast and cruises the high seas, often far north.

When mature he averages about twelve feet in length, he is a powerful swimmer and he is very bold.

Salient in his appearance is his long graceful form terminating in a head, less than a fourth of his body length and ending in a sharp-pointed snout.

Nostrils are nearer the large crescent-shaped mouth than to the end of the snout and it is to be noticed that the rear two of the five gill-openings are above the for-ward point of the pectorals.

Teeth are large, twenty-five upper front row, thirty-one, lower, alternating to form a continuous cutting edge and each tooth is curved slightly outward. The middle tooth of the lower row is small, all are finely serrate, those of the upper row being broad and triangular and those of the lower row blade-like.

Pectorals appear extremely long and narrow, length being twice the base. First dorsal, entirely forward of the middle of the fish, is longer than high, its front edge curved, its rear edge almost straight but with a narrow extension along the back. The

From Garman   *Courtesy of Museum of Comparative Zoology, Harvard*

CARCHARODON CARCHARIAS
(Great White Shark)

From Garman   *Courtesy of Museum of Comparative Zoology, Harvard*

CARCHARINIDAE AND ISURIDAE
Upper: *Carcharias taurus* (Sand Shark).
Lower: *Isurus punctatus* (Porbeagle—Similar to Mackerel).

From Garman   *Courtesy of Museum of Comparative Zoology, Harvard*

GALEUS GLAUCUS
(Great Blue Shark)

From Garman   *Courtesy of Museum of Comparative Zoology, Harvard*

CARCHARINIDAE
Upper: *Scoliodon terrae novae* (Sharp-nosed Shark).
Lower: *Carcharbinus limbatus* (Black-tipped Shark).

second dorsal has a base about half as long as the base of the first dorsal, its rear lower corner being much produced. Ventrals are small as is also the anal which is deeply notched on its back edge. Caudal moderate with very long upper lobe.

The color of this fish is dark blue or bluish-black on the back, shading to lighter blue and whitish below. There is no question of his being grey or brown for, at the first glance, he is a blue shark.

Besides the color, to identify this species, notice particularly the long pointed pectorals, the characteristic first dorsal, the notched anal and the teeth. Notice, too, the smoothly tapering body and the long pointed snout.

THE DUSKY SHARK
(*Carcharinus obscurus*)

THIS shark is essentially a fish-eater and is commonly pelagic but he also frequents bays and estuaries where he is more likely to be found than other pelagic species.

His fusiform body is stocky and thick, suggesting great power rather than speed. His rather short conical head terminates in a rounded blunt snout which is flattened at the forward edge. Teeth, thirty in upper row, twenty-nine, lower, are finely serrate; those of upper row, broad and inclined outward, those of lower row, lanceolate and erect.

A distinctive feature is the great length of the falciform pectorals, three times as long as broad and reaching back to the first dorsal. First dorsal is moderate in size but is much lower than that of the Brown (*C. milberti*), with which the Dusky might be confused, and the fin is placed further back than the dorsal of the Brown.

This shark frequently attains a length of more than ten feet and he is very heavy. Color, brownish-grey above, whitish below.

The Dusky is common all along our Atlantic coast, in the West Indies, in the Caribbean and in the Gulf of Mexico. He is powerful and has tremendous vitality but he is logy and slow on the line.

THE BROWN SHARK
(*Carcharinus milberti*)

THIS shark, common on our Atlantic seaboard, is a temperate zone species though found also in the tropics. Another name for him is New York Ground Shark.

His body is rather like that of the Dusky as is his head, with short, rounded, blunt snout.

[177]

TIGERS OF THE SEA

Teeth, twenty-five in upper front row, twenty-nine, lower, are finely serrate. Those of the upper row are broad, triangular and inclined slightly outward; lower, narrow and erect.

Length, about six or seven feet; color, greyish-brown above, lighter below, whitish on belly.

It is easy to confuse this shark with the Dusky but notice that his first dorsal is much higher, is curved on the back edge and is over practically the whole space between pectorals and ventrals. Also notice that the teeth of the Brown are 25/29 while the Dusky's are 30/29.

THE BLACK TIPPED SHARK
(*Carcharbinus limbatus*)

THIS species, abundant off Florida, in the Bahamas and throughout the Caribbean, appeals less to the shark-hunter than do larger sharks, for it rarely reaches six feet in length and, though rather game, the Black Tip is a mulish fighter.

He is slender of build with long pointed snout which is characteristically uptilted.

His first dorsal fin is moderate in size and triangular in shape. Pectorals are large and triangular. Caudal fin is long and narrow, the upper lobe being more than twice as long as the lower.

His teeth are long slender triangles, alike in both jaws but larger in the upper.

Color is grey with black tips on the fins. Belly is white.

THE SAND SHARK
(*Carcharias taurus*)

THIS is one of the commonest sharks of the estuaries of our Middle Atlantic seaboard. His usual length is perhaps five or six feet but he does attain twice that length. He is not a fast swimmer nor a game fighter but the uncertainty of his actions makes him interesting on the line.

He is slender in shape with extremely long and pointed snout. His first and second dorsal fins are triangular, the bases being about the same length as the front edges, their shorter back edges being curved. The pectorals and the ventrals are also short and broad. The caudal is narrow with extremely long upper lobe. The characteristic and unusual feature of this shark's fin equipment is, however, that the first and second dorsals are of almost the same size and that the large and almost rectangular ventrals are nearly the same size and shape of the small pectorals. The anal is almost as large as either of them.

His teeth are long narrow spikes, slightly curved and alike in both jaws.

His color is grey with indistinct spots on back and sides and his fins are edged with black. On the belly he is a yellowish-white.

THE HAMMERHEAD
(*Sphyrna zygaena*)

HAMMERHEADS show an interesting step of specialized development in the Plagiostomia in which there is a tendency toward flattening and broadening of the head. In skates and rays, where this broadening is highly emphasized, there are wing-like extensions from the trunk along practically its entire length which wings serve not only for propulsion but also to facilitate the fish in lying on the bottom.

With the Bonnethead (*Cestracion tiburo*) and the Hammerhead (*Sphyrna zygaena*) this widening has occurred only from about the mouth forward. With the Bonnethead the vanes are longer longitudinally (from front to back) and shorter laterally (from side to side) than they are with the Hammerhead and his head takes on the shape of a spade about three-quarters as long as wide.

With the Hammerhead the vanes extend from the snout to both sides, to about the width of the body. The front edge is roughly the segment of a circle with center at the fifth gill-slit and the parallel back edge reaches the body about at the corners of the mouth. With this freakish head and his slender body, the outline of the fish is exactly that of a blacksmith hammer on its helve.

While this vane, which may be regarded almost as a fin, is of no value for propulsion, it is of great value as a forward rudder, especially for vertical steering.

In both Bonnethead and Hammerhead the body is very slender and tapering. Snout, long and sharp. Mouth, crescent, narrow between tips.

Teeth, similar in both jaws but larger in upper. They are triangular, with slightly curved inner edge and deeply notched outer edge. All are finely serrate.

Pectorals, large and triangular with blunt points. First dorsal, very high, height much greater than base, its front origin back of pectoral base and its width about equal to one-fourth of the distance to the snout. Base of second dorsal half that of anal, above the middle of which the front origin sets. Caudal is nearly a third the length of the fish, its upper lobe three times as long as the lower.

Color, ashy-brown, shading to white beneath.

The eyes of these species, located in the outer ends of the vanes, are not small, amber and sinister as in most sharks but are large and cow-like.

The Hammerhead is a fast top-swimmer and a fish-eater and is common to most temperate and tropical seas. In addition to great speed, he is capable of quick maneuvers and he is one of the best sport-fish of the sharks.

He reaches a maximum length of eighteen feet but, being very slender, his weight is less than that of other sharks of the same length.

THE THRESHER SHARK
(*Alopias vulpes*)

THIS is a warm water species common, however, along our Atlantic coast, in summertime, as far north as New England. He seems to be particularly abundant about Block Island.

In color he is blackish above and pale below and he attains a length of fifteen feet.

He is easily distinguished by his long caudal fin, the upper lobe of which is about as long as head and body combined. This long whip-like tail he uses as a flail to splash water and herd fish into compact masses before dashing upon them.

He is a surface swimmer, fast, very nervous and very excitable. When in a pound he sometimes literally exhausts himself dashing around in frantic efforts to escape.

He is a great nuisance to fishermen through tearing their nets and pounds. He is frequently taken on the hook.

THE WHALE SHARK
(*Rhineodon typus*)

LITTLE is known of this largest and very rare species, not even as to his habits of breeding. Dr. E. W. Gudger, the authority on the Whale Shark, believes that it will be learned that the Whale Shark is viviparous though that is yet undetermined.

There are now but eighty-one records of the species, most of them taken about Florida, on the west coast of Mexico and in the Philippines.

In size, this shark is a whale, having been measured up to forty-five feet in length and estimated by scientific men, who cannot be doubted, up to sixty feet. His average is probably about thirty feet.

[180]

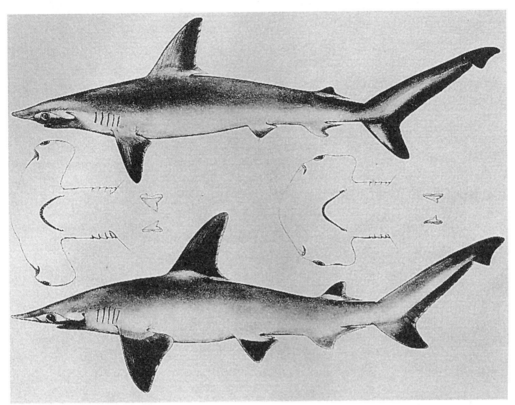

From Garman   *Courtesy of Museum of Comparative Zoology, Harvard*

CESTRACTIONTIDAE
Upper: *Sphyrna zygaena* (Hammerhead).
Lower: *Cestracion tiburo* (Bonnethead).

MUSTELUS CANIS
(Smooth Dogfish)

THRESHER SHARK
(*Alopias vulpes*)

SQUALUS ACANTHIAS
(Spiny Dogfish)

APPENDIX I

Like the whale, he feeds swimming along the surface with open mouth into which go small fishes, jellyfishes, crabs and algae. These are swallowed down a small throat after they are strained from huge volumes of water passed out through the gill-brushes.

The mouth of an average Whale Shark would easily take in a man and it is equipped with about six thousand teeth but these teeth are themselves evidence of the small creatures he devours for they are but an eighth of an inch long.

In spite of his fearsome appearance the Whale Shark is a mild-mannered creature which is never known to have attacked man though a wallop from his tail might easily crush a boat into matchwood and a man into pulp.

In color the Whale Shark is extremely beautiful. Along his dorsal ridge extends a line and three others, parallel to it, extend along his sides. Crossing these are vertical yellow or yellowish-white bars and in the squares so formed are large yellow spots.[1]

SMOOTH DOGFISH
(*Mustelus canis*)

SPINY DOGFISH
(*Squalus acanthias*)

THESE species are mentioned because they are both so abundant along our coast that the angler, out with light tackle after other fish, will be catching them anywhere between Cape Sable and Cape Cod, whether he wishes to catch them or not.

These little pests are rarely more than three feet in length, usually smaller, and, being slender, they are lightweights. They are fast swimmers, vigorous strikers and, at first, put up a game fight but they soon surrender. Nevertheless, when other fish are not biting and when the angler gets into a swarm of these little devils, he may have fine sport with light tackle.

Both of these species have typical shark heads and elongate fusiform bodies, flattened underneath.

Their color is brownish-grey on top shading to white on the belly. The Spiny has small spots on back and sides and he is also distinguished by sharp stiff spines on his dorsal fins.

Being largely crustacean-feeders their teeth are of the pavement type.

With us the dogfish is of no value but it is prejudice, alone, which prevents their boneless, tender palatable flesh from being popular as it is in England.

1. Gudger, E. W., *The Whale Shark*, Am. Mus. Natl. History, September, 1935.

APPENDIX II

TACKLE

IN this book there has to be such frequent reference to the equipment and tackle used that, for those persons who are not entirely familiar with deep-sea tackle, some explanation should be given.

With the very light tackles, such as are commonly used for trout, bass and grilse, the rod is usually of from two to four pieces, joints, the heaviest of which, the butt, carries the reel. This slender light rod is described by its material, its total length and its total weight. For example, we speak of a split-bamboo grilse rod, nine feet, five ounces, by which we mean that the total length of the rod, including butt, is nine feet and its total weight is five ounces.

Rods used for heavy sea fish, such as tarpon, tuna and swordfish, are usually of but two pieces, the short heavy butt whose length and weight are usually ignored, and the longer and more flexible tip, whose weight and length characterize the rod. We would, therefore, speak of a hickory swordfish rod with sixty-six inch, sixteen-ounce tip. Such a rod would be "heavy" tackle by the classification of fishing clubs which specify conditions for "heavy," "light" and "three-six" tackles.

Reels, ordinarily used for deep-sea fishing, multiply by two and a half the turns of the handle for the turn of the spindle. The size of the reels is from 1/0, with 3⅛ inch diameter of spool plate, to 16/0, with 8½ inch diameter of plate. Under the crank-handle, there is usually a star drag wheel for regulating the resistance of the outgoing line. There is, on the rim of the plate, a friction-drag for putting on a constant resistance, and there is a leather thumb-pad, for pressure upon the spool. By means of a lever, on the rim, drags may be instantly thrown off so the spindle may run free.

All this sounds very complicated and, as a matter of fact, it is complicated but all are necessary and only when practice has made the angler expert in the manipulation of these gadgets, can he properly handle the rushes of a big fish.

For salt water, linen line is generally considered best. Its size and strength are indicated by its number which is the number of strands laid in the line. Roughly, a good line bears a strain of two pounds for each strand, when dry, or three pounds, wet. Thus a No. 6 line, with six strands, bears twelve pounds, dry, or eighteen pounds, wet, and a No. 39 bears a hundred and seventeen pounds, wet.

While these may not seem strong enough to hold fish weighing more pounds than those tests, yet they are amply strong if the fish is properly handled for, in such case, no fish throws a strain upon the line of more than a rather small fraction of his weight. I have caught a nine hundred pound shark on a No. 30 line which bears a strain of but ninety pounds.

For big pelagic fish, hooks must, of course, be of finely tempered steel. Shapes of different makes vary from those with long shanks to those of decided pot-hook outline. Sizes are from 1/0 up to 14/0, which is about four inches long and about two and a half inches across the bend.

For strong-jawed, sharp-toothed fishes, there must be, next to the hook, a short length of small phosphor-bronze chain and, for fish which could cut the line with stiff fins or sandpaper it with denticled hide, there should be fifteen or twenty feet of wire leader, swivelled at both ends to prevent twisting.

A few feet of the line, next to the leader, is doubled back on itself, to give additional strength for the final struggle when the fish is brought to "iron."

The iron may be a heavy regular gaff-hook, or it may be a harpoon, a swordfish dart, or a horse-mackerel gaff, in all of which the head, when fast in the fish, detaches from the shaft and is held by a stout lanyard.

A killing-lance may be advisable to assure the death of large fish before they are taken into the boat.

To maintain the bait at a desired depth, a float may be attached to the line or leader.

The butt of the rod sets into a pivoting socket on the chair seat. A shoulder harness, like an open-front vest is fastened by straps to the reel and so holds the rod to the angler.

SPECIAL TACKLE FOR HEAVY SHARKS

Rod:—For big sharks I recommend a split-bamboo or a hickory rod but I prefer the hickory because, though more liable to take a set, it is tougher and more suitable than a built-up rod for the rough work required of it. The butt should be about twenty inches long, with heavy reel-seat and threaded reel-locking device. In the butt-cap there should be a slot to fit over the pin across the bottom of the rod-socket so the rod will not turn in the hands.

A long tip gives greater flexibility to the rod and so relieves jerks on the line. My tip is sixty-seven inches and its joint end is covered with felt to make it easier to hold. Guides, of non-corrosive metal, should sit close down on the rod and the offset tip-top

Killing   14/0   Swordfish
Lance   Grinnell   Dart
         Hook
12/0, 9/0, 6/0 Reels
Rod Seat

should be of the same material. There is no advantage in agate guides which are fragile and a nuisance.

REEL:—The reel has to take a severe beating and it has to be good. It must be remembered that any large reel is to be kept clean and well lubricated. The Edward vom Hofe, the Kovalovsky, and the Balboa reels have all given me good service. Size 12/0 carries a fishing-length of line of about 1200 feet of No. 36 or about 1500 feet of No. 30. Either of these lengths are enough and there is a disadvantage in too large a reel.

With any big reel there is danger of straining the plates and therefore it should be secured to the rod with a counter-brace.

LINE:—Cotton lines stretch, silk lines rot, so good hard-laid linen lines are best. All standard makes of these bear the manufacturer's guarantee of test strength. Lines come in olive, white and natural colour but I have never found much advantage in any colour though I usually use olive.

At the start of fishing, it is well to run out the line to get it wet because it is a third stronger that way. When a line is being used for several days, it is unnecessary to dry it each night but it should not be put away damp. A large slat reel on which to dry the line prevents it from kinking while drying.

Lines should be frequently examined for, expensive though they are, it is poor economy to use one with a flaw.

LEADER:—The wire leader must be long enough so the shark cannot reach the line with his teeth and so, by rolling, may not bring his denticled hide against it. It should therefore be fifteen or twenty feet long. Piano wire is stiff, liable to kink and hard to work. A stainless steel wire, available at tackle stores, obviates these disadvantages to some extent and it does not corrode. But a stainless steel cable (3/64 inch) made of twisted small wires is thoroughly satisfactory.

SWIVELS:—At the upper end of the leader there should be a swivel (I recommend "Siwash") to which the double line is tied with a bowline (not attached by a loop which will cut). To a swivel, at the lower end of the leader, is attached, by a No. 10 split ring, soldered, about ten inches of small phosphor-bronze chain to which is attached, by another ring, the hook.

HOOK:—There are a number of good hooks but I have had greatest success with Grinnell 14/0 and Zane Grey 13/0. The Grinnell 14/0 will stand the strain from the largest shark and a smaller one will have no trouble in getting it into his mouth.

The hook must be large to carry the large bait and its crook must be long enough to reach through the thick lips of the shark.

All of this gear has to be strong and, consequently, conspicuous so, doubtless, it may excite the suspicion of the shark. Therefore I sometimes camouflage the hook and chain by wrapping them loosely with seaweed.

ROD-RESTS—An objectionable feature of the rod-rests found in tackle stores is that they often have to be morticed into the chair seat and one does not always have a special fishing-chair available. I have, therefore, had one made which, while allowing universal movement of the rod, may be screwed onto any swivel chair or onto a thwart, and it can be carried along in the tackle box. Of course, some sort of rod-rest is absolutely indispensable.

FLOAT:—As good a float as any is a child's bright-coloured rubber play ball, about four inches in diameter, tied to line or leader where it will hold the bait at the desired depth.

THE IRON:—The regular swordfish dart is excellent. The detachable head should be mounted on an ash rake-handle for great length is unnecessary though weight is advisable. It requires power to drive the spear through the denticled hide but when the head is buried it will probably hold. The lanyard, three hundred feet of 3/16 inch rope, is coiled in a bucket. A heavy horse-mackerel gaff, with barbed point, and detachable head might be used or even a harpoon. Something of the sort is necessary because the fish could not be held with an ordinary gaff.

KILLING LANCE:—Before coming to very close quarters with a big shark, it is well to assure oneself that he is dead or at least beyond capability of doing harm. When he is brought on the line to the boatside, the boatman drives the dart into him. When he is again hauled in, this time on the lanyard, he gets the killing lance which is an army bayonet, sharpened on both edges and mounted on a stout staff.

TACKLE FOR BAHAMA TRIP—1935

Included to aid in assembling tackle for an expedition.

RODS

One Split Bamboo—Tip 68″, 13 oz.
One Hickory—Tip 73″, 17 oz. (One extra tip.)
One Hickory—Tip 72″, 10 oz.

One Split Bamboo—Tip 55″, 8 oz.
Two Split Bamboo—Tip 54″, 5 oz.

REELS

One Kovalovsky 14/0.
One Balboa 12/0.
One vom Hofe 9/0.
One vom Hofe 6/0.
Two Ocean City 2/0.
One Norka 1/0.

LINES

No. 36, Four lines, 1200 ft. each.
Two lines, 800 ft. each.
No. 30, Two lines, 900 ft. each.
No. 24, Two lines, 1200 ft. each.
No. 18, Two lines, 600 ft. each.
No. 12, Two lines, 600 ft. each.
No. 9, Two lines, 600 ft. each.
85 lb. test cod-line, two lines, 300 ft. each.
3/16 inch Manila Rope, two 300 ft. coils, for lanyards.

LEADERS

Six 20′, 3/64″, stainless steel cable, swivelled.
Six 20′, 156 lb. test, stainless steel wire, swivelled.
Twelve 3′ phosphor-bronze, 53 lb. test, swivelled.
Six 3′, light phosphor-bronze, swivelled.

HOOKS

Six 14/0 Grinnell.
Six 13/0 Zane Grey.
Six 14/0 Mustad.
Six 14/0 Norwegian.
Six 12/0 Mustad.
Six 12/0 Norwegian.
Twelve 10/0 vom Hofe.

Twelve 9/0 vom Hofe.
Assorted hooks 6/0 and 8/0.
Two large hand-line hooks on chains.

LURES
Twenty-four assorted lures and jigs.

MISCELLANEOUS
Sinkers.
Connecting Links.
Split Rings.
Swivels.
Coil of stainless leader wire (156 lb. test).
Coil of phosphor-bronze leader wire (50 lb. test).

LUBRICANT, ETC.
Oil.
Gear Grease.
Wax.
Cement.
Rod Varnish.

TOOLS
Knife.
Pliers.
Screwdriver.
File.
Small Hammer.
Carborundum.
Sandpaper.
Needles and Thread.
Small Copper Wire.
Pins.
Screw Hooks.
Rags.
Tire Tape.

[188]

APPENDIX II

EQUIPMENT

    Swordfish Dart and Extra Heads.
    Heavy Gaff-Hook.
    Killing Lance.
    Bolo.
    Float Balls.
    Shoulder Harness.
    Rod-Rests.
    Goggles.

FIRST AID

    First Aid Kit.
    Unguentine.
    Iodine.
    Drybak.
    Adhesive Tape.